A Note From Rick Renner

I am on a personal quest to see a "revival of the Bible" so people can establish their lives on a firm foundation that will stand strong and endure the test when the end-time storm winds begin to intensify.

In order to experience a revival of the Bible in your personal life, it is important to take time each day to read, receive, and apply its truths to your life. James tells us that if we will continue in the perfect law of liberty — refusing to be forgetful hearers but determined to be doers — we will be blessed in our ways. As you watch or listen to the programs in this series and work through this corresponding study guide, I trust that you will search the Scriptures and allow the Holy Spirit to help you hear something new from God's Word that applies specifically to your life. I encourage you to be a doer of the Word that He reveals to you. Whatever the cost, I assure you — it will be worth it.

> Thy words were found, and I did eat them;
> and thy word was unto me the joy and rejoicing of mine heart:
> for I am called by thy name, O Lord God of hosts.
> — Jeremiah 15:16

Your brother and friend in Jesus Christ,

Rick Renner

Unless otherwise indicated, all scripture quotations are taken from the *King James Version* of the Bible.

Scripture quotations marked (*NKJV*) are taken from the *New King James Version*®. Copyright © 1982 by Thomas Nelson. Used by permission. All rights reserved.

Scripture quotations marked (*NLT*) are taken from the *Holy Bible*, N*ew Living Translation*, copyright © 1996, 2004, 2015 by Tyndale House Foundation. Used by permission of Tyndale House Publishers, Inc., Carol Stream, Illinois 60188. All rights reserved.

Unknown Facts About the Death, Burial, and Resurrection of Jesus Christ

Copyright © 2019 by Rick Renner
8316 E. 73rd St.
Tulsa, Oklahoma 74133

Published by Rick Renner Ministries
www.renner.org

ISBN 13: 978-1-68031-629-2

eBook ISBN 13: 978-1-68031-667-4

All rights reserved. No portion of this book may be reproduced or transmitted in any form or by any means — electronic, mechanical, photocopy, recording, scanning, or other — except for brief quotations in critical reviews or articles, without the prior written permission of the Publisher.

How To Use This Study Guide

This 25-lesson study guide corresponds to *"Unknown Facts About the Death, Burial, and Resurrection of Jesus Christ" With Rick Renner* (Renner TV). Each lesson in this guide covers a topic that is addressed during the program series, with questions and references supplied to draw you deeper into your own private study of the Scriptures on this subject.

To derive the most benefit from this study guide, consider the following:

First, watch or listen to the program prior to working through the corresponding lesson in this guide. (Programs can also be viewed at **renner.org** by clicking on the Media/Archives links.)

Second, take the time to look up the scriptures included in each lesson. Prayerfully consider their application to your own life.

Third, use a journal or notebook to make note of your answers to each lesson's Study Questions and Practical Application challenges.

Fourth, invest specific time in prayer and in the Word of God to consult with the Holy Spirit. Write down the scriptures or insights He reveals to you about being filled with the Spirit and empowered by Him in your daily life.

Finally, take action! Whatever the Lord tells you to do according to His Word, do it.

For added insights on this subject, it is recommended that you obtain Rick Renner's book *Paid in Full — An In-depth Look at the Defining Moments of Christ's Passion*. You can also select from Rick's other available resources by placing your order at **renner.org** or by calling 1-800-742-5593.

LESSON 1

TOPIC
Wounds of Betrayal

SCRIPTURES
1. **John 12:1-8** — Then Jesus six days before the passover came to Bethany, where Lazarus was which had been dead, whom he raised from the dead. There they made him a supper; and Martha served: but Lazarus was one of them that sat at the table with him. Then took Mary a pound of ointment of spikenard, very costly, and anointed the feet of Jesus, and wiped his feet with her hair: and the house was filled with the odour of the ointment. Then saith one of his disciples, Judas Iscariot, Simon's son, which should betray him, Why was not this ointment sold for three hundred pence, and given to the poor? This he said, not that he cared for the poor; but because he was a thief, and had the bag, and bare what was put therein. Then said Jesus, Let her alone: against the day of my burying hath she kept this. For the poor always ye have with you; but me ye have not always.
2. **John 13:2** —And supper being ended, the devil having now put into the heart of Judas Iscariot, Simon's son, to betray him.

GREEK WORDS
1. "put into" — (*ballo*): to throw, cast, thrust, or inject; carries the idea of a very fast action of throwing, thrusting, or injecting something, such as the throwing of a ball or rock, or the forward thrusting of a sharp knife

SYNOPSIS
The 25 lessons in this study on ***Unknown Facts About the Death, Burial, and Resurrection of Jesus Christ*** will focus on the following topics:

- Wounds of Betrayal
- Agony of the Soul
- Divine Assistance
- How Many Soldiers Does It Take To Arrest One Man?

- Misunderstandings and Suspicions
- Kiss of Deception
- Test of Loyalty, Test of Love
- Paralyzed by His Presence
- The Danger of Taking Matters Into Your Own Hands
- Jesus Cleans Up Peter's Mess
- Twelve Legions of Angels
- Who Is the Naked Boy in the Garden of Gethsemane?
- Has Anyone Ever Spit in Your Face?
- Playing Games at Jesus' Expense
- Surrender and Release Yourself Into the Loving Care of God
- Pilate Looks for a Loophole
- Herod Meets Jesus
- A Human Ruler Mocks the King of Kings and Lord of Lords
- Charged, but Not Guilty
- The Horror of a Roman Scourging
- Crucified!
- It Is Finished!
- Buried and Sealed
- Behold, He Is Risen!
- An Empty Tomb!

The emphasis of this lesson:

Judas Iscariot betrayed Jesus Christ. Through the doorway of offense, Satan entered into Judas' heart and destroyed not only his relationship with Jesus, but also Judas' very life. Betrayal is a painful experience. In this lesson, you'll learn how a person becomes a betrayer and what you can do to avoid this deadly trap.

Understanding Betrayal

When someone betrays you, it can feel as if that person has put a knife into your heart and twisted it. The pain is intense because it usually comes from someone you are close to — someone you love and trust deeply. This is often a person you walk with, talk with, and even pray with who abruptly turns against you and becomes an enemy.

When you are betrayed, if you focus on the betrayal and the pain it produces, it will only deepen the hurt. You will become bitter, numb, and isolated from others.

The truth is, in a situation of betrayal, you are not the only victim. The person who betrayed you is a victim too. Somehow Satan penetrated that person's mind and emotions with his lies, and he or she is no longer thinking or seeing things accurately. A demonic, outside force has tainted the way that individual see things, negatively influencing his or her perception.

When you've been betrayed and you're able to understand that you're not the only victim — and that the enemy has taken your betrayer captive — it will help you have compassion on that other person. This is how Jesus saw Judas Iscariot's deadly betrayal.

How Judas Became a Betrayer

When we think of betrayal, the first person many of us think of is Judas Iscariot. He was one of the Twelve — a close, inner-circle, confidant of Jesus Himself. Judas interacted with Jesus on a regular basis. He was the ministry's treasurer, and as such, he and Jesus no doubt had many close conversations about ministry, money, and life. Judas was a part of all the miracles, healings, and deliverances that occurred in Jesus' ministry on the earth.

How could someone so intimately connected with Christ become a betrayer? The answer is simple: Judas became *offended* at Jesus.

When a person becomes offended, it is as if he puts on a new set of glasses, and the lenses of those glasses expose all the things about the other person he dislikes. Suddenly, he can no longer see anything good about that person. All he can see are faults, flaws, and places where they disagree.

If you are experiencing this kind of perception of someone in your life, it is a sure sign the devil is working on your mind. The word "Satan" is the Greek word *satanas*, which means *accuser*. When you hear recurring accusing thoughts about others in your mind and you begin to agree with those thoughts, you are actually agreeing with the enemy.

When you begin to experience a flood of negative thoughts and emotions toward someone, you need to put a halt to the enemy's work. Surrender and submit yourself to God (*see* James 4:7). In this position of humility, you can take authority over the devil as well as your mind, will, and emotions (*see* Luke 10:19). You can fight off the enemy's efforts to turn you into a betrayer.

The Devil Is the Destroyer of Relationships

Before time began, Satan was at work attempting to destroy relationships. Once iniquity was found in his heart and before he was kicked out of Heaven, Lucifer worked deceptively behind the scenes sowing seeds of discord, confusion, and strife among the angels. In that perfect environment, his slanderous accusations negatively influenced one third of those angels to rebel against God and join forces with him.

After God hurled Satan and his rebellious cohorts out of Heaven, mankind became Satan's next target. As a serpent in the garden of Eden, Satan whispered his slanderous accusations against God to Eve. She and Adam swallowed his lies, and their relationship with God was broken. Adam betrayed God. Then we know that Cain betrayed Abel, Absalom betrayed David, and on and on through history the list of betrayal goes.

The devil is a pro at creating discord, confusion, and strife. He stealthily lures people into being offended at others — even at God. Little by little, he feeds them one accusation after another, getting them to fixate on another's weaknesses, failures, and points of disagreement. The longer his work goes undetected, the more human relationships he is able to destroy.

Think about it. Angels who once stood in the very presence of God, worshiping Him in Heaven for eons of time, bought Satan's slanderous accusations against the Most High. The devil was so persuasive that these mighty supernatural beings turned against God. How much easier do you think it is for him to persuade human beings to give in to his lies?

The Devil Turned Judas Into a Betrayer

Satan got a foothold into Judas' life through offense. We see this outlined in John 12:1-8.

> Then Jesus six days before the passover came to Bethany, where Lazarus was which had been dead, whom he raised from the dead. There they made him a supper; and Martha served: but Lazarus was one of them that sat at the table with him. Then took Mary a pound of ointment of spikenard, very costly, and anointed

the feet of Jesus, and wiped his feet with her hair: and the house was filled with the odour of the ointment. (vv. 1-3)

The value of the ointment was about one year's wages. It was extremely expensive.

Then saith one of his disciples, Judas Iscariot, Simon's son, which should betray him, Why was not this ointment sold for three hundred pence, and given to the poor? This he said, not that he cared for the poor; but because he was a thief, and had the bag, and bare what was put therein. (vv. 4-6)

Judas was the treasurer for Jesus' ministry. In his opinion, what Mary had done with the ointment was a waste, and he took issue with Jesus for allowing her to do it. In reality, Judas had no right to take issue with Jesus. Nevertheless, he did and this was the turning point in his life — the point at which Satan gained entrance to his heart. In response to Judas' accusations, Jesus said, "...Let her alone: against the day of my burying hath she kept this. For the poor always ye have with you; but me ye have not always" (vv. 7, 8). Prophetically, Jesus was declaring that Mary was anointing Him for His burial. His statement was true. They would always have poor people, but they would only have Him for a few more days.

Try to imagine this scenario from Judas' point of view. He was a thief in charge of the ministry's money. He watched as ointment valued at an entire year's income was used up in minutes. Add to this the fact that the Miracle-Worker he admired and saw as the answer to overthrowing Roman oppression just sat there, approving of what appeared to be a total waste of resources. How would you have responded had you been in Judas' shoes?

We know how Judas responded. He disagreed with Jesus' use of resources. He also likely thought Jesus' response to him was arrogant. In that very moment, Judas became offended at Jesus. When he did, a doorway to his heart opened, and the devil quickly injected a seed of betrayal.

This is made clear in John 13:2. Just a few days later, Jesus was with His disciples eating the Passover meal together in the Upper Room. After He had washed their feet and served them Communion, the Bible says, "And supper being ended, the devil having now put into the heart of Judas Iscariot, Simon's son, to betray him."

The phrase "put into" is from the Greek word *ballo*, which means *to throw, to cast, to thrust, or to inject*. It carries the idea of *a very fast action of throwing, thrusting, or injecting something forward like a ball, a rock, or a sharp knife*.

That part of John 13:2 could actually be translated: *"The devil now having thrust into the heart of Judas Iscariot,"* or, *"The devil now having inserted into the heart of Judas Iscariot,"* or even, *"The devil now having forcibly hurled or imbedded into the heart of Judas Iscariot."*

The word *ballo* ("put into") also indicates how quickly the devil acted. It was like a flash of lightning. The moment offense opened the door into Judas' heart, Satan immediately injected his seed of betrayal. It became imbedded, lodging and festering inside of Judas. Instead of dealing with his wrong thoughts and taking them captive, Judas nurtured the offense, and it conceived and gave birth to the betrayal of Jesus Christ.

STUDY QUESTIONS

Study to shew thyself approved unto God, a workman that needeth not to be ashamed, rightly dividing the word of truth.
— 2 Timothy 2:15

1. In your own words, briefly describe what Satan does to get a person to open his or her heart so he can sow into that person's heart a seed of betrayal.
2. According to God's Word, how important is it for you to willingly release the offenses of others? What will happen if you choose to hold on to unforgiveness toward those who hurt you? (Consider Matthew 6:14, 15; Mark 11:24, 25; Ephesians 4:26, 27, 31, 32; and Colossians 3:12, 13.)
3. Think about it. Is someone offended with *you*? Is he or she holding unforgiveness toward you and you're not sure why? Carefully read Jesus' words in Matthew 5:23, 24 and describe the course of action He wants you to take in such situations.

PRACTICAL APPLICATION

But be ye doers of the word, and not hearers only, deceiving your own selves.
— James 1:22

1. The first step to betrayal is to become *offended* at someone and unwilling to release the hurt to God. When you're offended, it is as if you put on glasses that only let you see a person's faults and failures. Satan then feeds you one accusation after another to deepen the wound and strengthen his hold on your life. Think about it. Is there someone in your life right now with whom you are offended? If so, who? What accusations has the enemy repeatedly brought to your mind about this person?
2. In his early years of ministry, Rick became offended with his pastor and mentor. God told Rick he would not go any further in his ministry until he apologized and asked for his forgiveness. What is the Holy Spirit speaking to you about the leaders He has placed in *your* life? Is there someone you need to go to and make things right with? Don't wait any longer. Obey what the Lord is prompting you to do, and you'll begin to experience His blessings once again.
3. Has someone you know turned against you? That person's heart was once warm and loving, but now his attitude has soured toward you? If so, you can know that he or she is under the enemy's influence. Pause and pray for that person right now. "Lord, give me compassion for [*insert person's name*]. I choose to release and forgive _____, and I ask You to deliver _____ from the enemy's trap of offense, in Jesus' name." (*See* 2 Timothy 2:25, 26.)

LESSON 2

TOPIC
Agony of the Soul

SCRIPTURES

1. **Luke 22:42** — Saying, Father, if thou be willing, remove this cup from me: nevertheless not my will, but thine, be done.
2. **Luke 22:44** — And being in an agony he prayed more earnestly: and his sweat was as it were great drops of blood falling down to the ground.
3. **Hebrews 2:18** — For in that he himself hath suffered being tempted, he is able to succour them that are tempted.

GREEK WORDS

1. "agony" — (*agonia*): an intense conflict or contest; a struggle; a fight; great exertion or effort; often used to convey the ideas of anguish, pain, distress, or conflict; comes from the word (*agon*), which depicted the athletic conflicts and competitions that were so famous in the ancient world; frequently pictured wrestlers in a match, with each wrestler struggling with all his might to overcome his opponent in an effort to hurl him to the ground in a fight to the finish; used figuratively to describe a struggle of the human will
2. "earnestly" — (*ektenes*): extended or stretched out; a person in this kind of agony might drop to the ground, writhing in pain, rolling this way and that way; pictures a person who is pushed to the limit and can't be stretched much more; a person on the brink of all he can possibly endure
3. "drops" — µ (*thrombos*): a medical word that points to blood that is unusually thickly clotted
4. "succour" — (*boetheo*): originally a military word to describe a soldier coming to the aid of another solider who was in trouble

SYNOPSIS

The size of the garden of Gethsemane in Jesus' day was much larger than the traditional, gated site we see today. Originally, Gethsemane covered the entire slope of the Mount of Olives. Some believe that the olive trees in Gethsemane today were sprouted from the very trees that were there 2,000 years ago when Jesus visited this garden with His disciples.

It was in this garden that Christ regularly pulled away to pray with His disciples. It is the place He visited the night He was betrayed. If there was ever a time Jesus needed the disciples' moral and spiritual support, it was on that night. Indeed, Jesus was in great *agony of soul*.

The emphasis of this lesson:

In Gethsemane, Jesus experienced an intense agony of the soul. Mentally and emotionally, He was pushed to the limit of all that a human being could endure. Writhing in mental and emotional pain, His will wrestled against the will of the Father. The internal fight was so severe, He began to sweat drops of blood. It was in the garden that He won the war against His will and completely submitted to the cross of Calvary.

For three years, Jesus was readily available to His disciples. He provided for all their needs, protected them from every enemy, made them partners in ministry, and answered their questions. There is no record in Scripture of Him ever needing their support, except for on the night He was betrayed.

Jesus knew what lie before Him — the beatings, the ridicule, the cross, and the grave. In His humanity, He needed the emotional, mental, and spiritual support of His friends. So He took Peter, James, and John — the three closest to Him — and pulled away, asking them to pray. But they fell asleep on the job. When Jesus needed them most, He was left alone in great agony.

They Love You — They Just Don't Understand

When we need the emotional, mental, and spiritual support of our friends, and they fail to come to our aid, it is usually not out of malicious intent. Most of the time, those who disappoint us do so because they don't fully comprehend what we're going through. Although they see we're having a difficult time and want to support us, they just don't understand what we're feeling inside.

Such was the case for Jesus on that night of desperation in Gethsemane. Peter, James, and John knew that Jesus was struggling and they wanted to help Him. However, they didn't comprehend the full weight of what Jesus was facing. They still didn't grasp that He was going to be crucified. They had no idea He was going to die and be in hell for three days. If they had really understood, they probably would have been more attentive and would not have fallen asleep.

When people feel abandoned by their friends and family during hard times, it is most likely true that it's not personal. Those friends and loved ones are not purposely trying to abandon those who are in trouble. They just don't comprehend the depth of what those people are going through. Those friends and family are probably doing the best they can.

Jesus *Writhed in Agony*

In the gospel of Luke, we find out how intense it was for Jesus the night He was betrayed in the garden of Gethsemane. As a physician, Luke often used medical terms to describe what was happening, and Luke 22:44 is a perfect example. It says, "And being in an agony he prayed more earnestly: and his sweat was as it were great drops of blood falling down to the ground."

The word "agony" is the Greek word *agonia*. It describes *an intense conflict or contest; a struggle or a fight*; or *great exertion or effort*. This word was often used to convey the idea of *anguish, pain, distress, or conflict*. It comes from the word *agon*, which depicted *the athletic conflicts and competitions that were so famous in the ancient world*. The word *agon* frequently pictured wrestlers in a match, with each wrestler struggling with all his might to overcome his opponent and hurl him to the ground in a fight to the finish. Figuratively, *agon* is used to describe *a struggle of the human will*.

When Jesus was in the garden that night, He knew what was ahead — the beatings, the cross, the grave, and separation from the Father. His heart and His head were in a fierce wrestling match. In His heart, Jesus knew and desired to do the will of the Father: to go to the cross and pay the penalty for mankind's sin, restoring their relationship with the Father. It was the reason He had been born. However, in Christ's humanity, His will was naturally to avoid the cross. Who in their right mind would want to be crucified on a cross? Who would want to die and spend three days in hellish torment?

Indeed, Jesus was in agony — He was literally in the fight of His life. Three times that night He prayed, "…Father, if thou be willing, remove this cup from me: nevertheless not my will, but thine, be done" (Luke 22:42). This is also recorded in Matthew 26:37-45 and Mark 14:35-41. Again and again, Christ's human will wrestled against the Father's will.

Gethsemane was a place of great conflict for Jesus. It is the place where the battle to submit to the cross of Calvary was won. Through God's strength, Jesus was finally able to come to the place of total surrender to the Father's will. But it was not without first experiencing great agony.

Jesus *Prayed More Earnestly*

In Luke 22:44, Luke went on to say that Jesus "…being in an agony he prayed more *earnestly*…." When you read this, you may think it means He prayer more fervently, but that's not what it means. The word "earnestly" is the Greek word *ektenes*, which is a medical term that means *to be extended or stretched out*. A person in this kind of agony might *drop to the ground, writhing in pain, rolling this way and that way*. So the word "earnestly" pictures *a person who is pushed to the limit of all that can be physically or mentally endured.* That person has gone as far as he can go and simply can't be stretched anymore.

By using the word *ektenes*, Luke the physician gives us a much different picture of Jesus in the garden of Gethsemane than some of the modern paintings show. Many of these render Jesus as reverently kneeling down, His hands clasped in prayer, and His elbows resting on a rock. The truth is, it wasn't like that at all. Jesus was in agony — He was on the ground, rolling around, and moving from side to side in great mental and emotional anguish. He was holding Himself and crying out to God, desperate for His help in the situation. That is an accurate picture of what the Scripture means when it says, "…he prayed more *earnestly*.…"

Jesus *Sweat Great Drops of Blood*

Looking at Luke 22:44 again, we read, "And being in an agony he prayed more earnestly: and his sweat was as it were great drops of blood falling down to the ground." The word "drops" is from the Greek word *thrombos*, which is *a medical term that points to blood that is unusually thickly clotted.* This reveals a rare, but very real medical condition that still exists in the world today.

Interestingly, the *Journal of the American Medical Association* (*JAMA*) published an article by a group of doctors who analyzed what happened to Jesus in the garden of Gethsemane. The article concluded that Jesus experienced a real medical condition. His mind and emotions were under such severe stress that His brain began to send signals to His body telling it that He was under physical pressure. That is, His mind perceived the stress as real, physical pressure, and it told His body to respond to it accordingly.

When this type of intense pressure occurs, the body responds in the following way: the top layer of skin separates from the second layer of skin, creating a vacuum. The vacuum then fills with blood. Since the person suffering is already profusely sweating from the intense pressure, the abundant pool of blood begins to mingle with the sweat and starts oozing through the pores of the skin.

We know that Jesus was in *agonia* — *a fierce wrestling match* between His human will and the Father's will. He prayed more "earnestly" — the Greek word *ektenes*, indicating *He was on the ground, writhing in pain, rolling this way and that way.* What Jesus experienced was beyond what any normal human being would ever endure. He was pushed to the limit emotionally, mentally, physically, and spiritually, knowing all that lay ahead of Him. Thus, He began to sweat great drops of blood.

Given this medical condition, we can determine that *before* Jesus left the garden of Gethsemane, He was already a bloody mess! It's no wonder He desperately yearned for the mental, emotional, and spiritual support of Peter, James, and John. Yet He was left to deal with the prospect of the cross on His own.

Jesus Is the Great Soldier Who Will Come to Your Aid and Stand by You!

If you are facing a very difficult situation in your life and you feel as though everyone has abandoned you, Jesus knows how you feel. When He needed the moral, emotional, and spiritual support of the people closest to Him, they failed to rise to the occasion.

The good news is, even if everyone else abandons you during your time of great difficulty, Jesus will always be present! Hebrews 2:18 declares, "For in that he himself hath suffered being tempted, he is able to succour them that are tempted."

The word "succour" is the Greek term *boetheo*. This was originally a military word used to describe *a soldier coming to the aid of another solider who was in trouble*. In other words, Jesus is a soldier who has been through the battles you're facing and knows what it's like to face them alone. If anyone understands you, He does. If you will cry out to Him when you're in trouble — whether it's a fiery trial or a riveting temptation — the Soldier of all soldiers, Jesus Christ Himself, will quickly rush to your aid!

STUDY QUESTIONS

Study to shew thyself approved unto God, a workman that needeth not to be ashamed, rightly dividing the word of truth.
— 2 Timothy 2:15

1. If you're facing a difficult situation in your life and you feel as though everyone has abandoned you, what can you remind yourself about your family and friends to help you *not* become offended with them? (Also consider Jesus' response in Luke 23:34.)

2. One of the greatest promises from the Lord is that He'll never leave you. Take some time to meditate on these passages proclaiming this truth. Write out the one that energizes you most. (*See* Matthew 28:20; John 10:28, 29; Isaiah 41:10; 43:2; Hebrews 13:5, 6.)
3. Carefully read Hebrews 2:18. How does this verse about Jesus and the meaning of the word "succour" encourage you in the midst of your trials and temptations?

PRACTICAL APPLICATION

> But be ye doers of the word, and not hearers only, deceiving your own selves.
> —James 1:22

1. Luke 22:44 says that Jesus, "being in an agony he prayed more earnestly: and his sweat was as it were great drops of blood falling down to the ground." After reading through this lesson and hearing the truth about what Christ went through for *you* in the garden of Gethsemane, how has your love and devotion for Him been affected and changed?
2. Are you experiencing a time of intense struggle? Has the Lord asked you to do something, and your human will is fighting to have its own way? If so, briefly explain the situation. Then pray and invite the Holy Spirit to empower you to submit your will to His will and to do what He's asking you to do.

LESSON 3

TOPIC
Divine Assistance

SCRIPTURES

1. **Luke 22:41-44** — And he was withdrawn from them about a stone's cast, and kneeled down, and prayed, saying, Father, if thou be willing, remove this cup from me: nevertheless not my will, but thine, be done. And there appeared an angel unto him from heaven, strengthening

him. And being in an agony he prayed more earnestly: and his sweat was as it were great drops of blood falling down to the ground.
2. **Mark 14:42** — Rise up, let us go; lo, he that betrayeth me is at hand.
3. **Hebrews 1:14** — Are they [angels] not all ministering spirits, sent forth to minister for them who shall be heirs of salvation?
4. **Hebrews 2:18** — For in that he himself hath suffered being tempted, he is able to succour them that are tempted.

GREEK WORDS

1. "earnestly" — (*ektenes*): extended or stretched out; a person in this kind of agony might drop to the ground, writhing in pain, rolling this way and that way; pictures a person who is pushed to the limit and can't be stretched much more; a person on the brink of all he can possibly endure
2. "drops" — μ (*thrombos*): a medical word that points to blood that is unusually thickly clotted
3. "strengthened" — (*enischuo*): to impart strength; to empower someone; to fill a person with heartiness; to give someone a renewed vitality; a person may have been feeling exhausted and depleted, but when he is "strengthened," he suddenly gets a blast of energy so robust that he is instantly recharged
4. "succour" — (*boetheo*): originally a military word to describe a soldier coming to the aid of another solider who was in trouble

SYNOPSIS

The traditional site known today as the garden of Gethsemane is significantly smaller in size than the garden's perimeters in Jesus' day. It was to this secluded place that He and His disciples came on the night He was betrayed. In great agony, Jesus prayed to the Father to let the cup of suffering pass from Him. Ultimately, He surrendered His will to the Father's will, and He received divine assistance to carry out His mission on the cross of Calvary.

The emphasis of this lesson:

Overwhelmed by all that lay before Him, Jesus was in great agony of soul the night He was betrayed in Gethsemane. Again and again, He cried out to the Father, and His prayers were heard. God gave Him supernatural strength to victoriously carry out His assignment.

Jesus *Collapsed Under the Weight* of the Situation

Just a short time after Jesus and His disciples shared their last supper in the Upper Room, they went to the garden of Gethsemane. Except for Judas Iscariot, all the disciples were with Him. He took Peter, James, and John a little farther away from the others and asked them to pray with Him. He desperately needed their emotional and spiritual support. He then went a little farther on His own and began to pray. The Bible says, "And he was withdrawn from them about a stone's cast, and kneeled down, and prayed" (Luke 22:41).

On the surface, this verse sounds like Jesus calmly and reverently kneeled down, and a "holy hush" came over Him. But that is not what happened. In the original Greek, the verse says, "He *collapsed.*" Jesus probably intended to go farther away from Peter, James, and John. However, He was already feeling the pressure and weight of what was about to take place. Unable to take another step, He collapsed. He fell on His hands and knees and began to cry out, "…Father, if thou be willing, remove this cup from me: nevertheless not my will, but thine, be done" (Luke 22:42).

Interestingly, the verb tense of the word "saying" here indicates a repeated activity. It means Jesus kept *saying* and *saying* and *saying* His request to God. In Matthew 26:39-44, it is recorded that He prayed three times, "…Father, if it be possible, let this cup pass from me: nevertheless not as I will, but as thou wilt" (v. 39). In His humanity, Jesus didn't want to drink that cup of suffering. The scourging, the crucifixion, and three days in the grave, including time in hell, was a horrific series of events to endure.

In His heart, Jesus knew that the cross and all it included was the will of the Father, and His heart wanted to do the Father's will. Yet His mind kept screaming, *Don't do it! It will be too torturous and painful! There MUST be another way!*

Jesus *Agonized in the Garden*

Luke 22:44 says, "And being in an agony he prayed more earnestly: and his sweat was as it were great drops of blood falling down to the ground." We saw in the last lesson, the word "agony" is the Greek word *agonia*, which describes *a contest or wrestling match*. Each wrestler tries to pin the other wrestler down on the mat and claim a resounding victory. But in this case, the wrestling match was between Jesus' will and the will of the Father. That night in Gethsemane, Jesus was in the fight of His life to pin His own will to the mat and surrender completely to the Father.

"And being in agony he prayed more earnestly...." The word "earnestly" is the Greek word *ektenes*, which describes *a person who is fully stretched out and extended to the point of what he can possibly tolerate.* This word depicts *a person undergoing more stress than a human being should be allowed to undergo — a person under intense pressure and agony who is lying on the ground, holding himself as he rolls around, writhing in pain.*

These moments in Gethsemane were moments of intense passion. In fact, they were so intense, Luke recorded that Jesus' "...sweat was as it were great *drops* of blood falling down to the ground" (v. 44).

The word "drops" is the Greek word *thrombos*, and it describes *thickly clotted blood.* The medical condition Christ experienced is one that still exists today. It occurs when a person comes under such intense mental, emotional, and spiritual pressure that his brain begins to send response signals to the entire body. The pressure perceived is so strong that the top layer of the person's skin separates from the second layer of skin, forming a vacuum. The vacuum then fills with blood, and instead of just normal sweat pouring out, *blood* begins to ooze from the person's pores.

That is what happened to Jesus the night He was praying in Gethsemane. *The Journal of the American Medical Association* confirms this. Writhing in pain, rolling on the ground, Jesus struggled to embrace the Father's plan. The pressure was so intense, He began to sweat blood. This lets us know that before Jesus was ever scourged by Pilate, He was already a bloody mess.

Peter, James, and John Were Clueless

Remember, Jesus had asked Peter, James, and John — the disciples closest to Him — to pray with Him. However, instead of praying, they went to sleep. The truth is, even though Jesus had told them He would suffer at the hands of the Jewish leaders and die on the cross, they didn't understand Him. They didn't comprehend the scourging He would face, nor did they realize He would spend three days in hell. They just didn't get it. Had the disciples really understood what Jesus was going to face, they probably would have stayed awake and faithfully prayed.

If it seems as if your friends have abandoned you in your time of trouble, don't take it personally. In their hearts, they probably really care about you and want to help. The reason they seem disconnected is, they don't understand the intensity of what you're going through or the weight of what you're feeling.

With God's help, Jesus was able to realize this about His disciples and avoid being offended at them. And if *you* have been hurt and are holding a grudge against a family member or friend because that person seems to have abandoned you, I encourage you to let it go. Release that person and you'll release *yourself*.

When others fail to stand with you like you think they should, realize they probably don't understand what you're going through. If they did, they would probably be faithfully supporting you. You can choose to forgive them and refuse to be offended by their actions or their seeming indifference toward you.

God Supernaturally Strengthened Jesus

Although the disciples didn't understand what Jesus was going through, God did. And He provided Him with divine assistance right in the midst of His suffering.

As Jesus was crying out in agony to the Father, the Scripture says, "And there appeared an angel unto him from heaven, strengthening him" (Luke 22:43). The word "strengthened" is the Greek word *enischuo*, which means *to impart strength* or *to empower someone*. It signifies *filling a person with hardiness, giving them a renewed vitality*. This person may have been feeling exhausted and depleted, but when he is "strengthened," he suddenly gets a blast of energy so robust that he is instantly recharged and ready to face the test or assignment before him.

God the Father provided this kind of supernatural strength for Jesus in Gethsemane that night. In Christ's time of intense struggle, divine assistance was imparted, renewing His strength and giving Him the energy and courage He needed to victoriously face the suffering that awaited Him.

Immediately after Christ was strengthened by the angel, He got up from that place and woke up the disciples. Mark 14:42 says He told them, "Rise up, let us go; lo, he that betrayeth me is at hand."

When you're in the midst of severe trouble or temptation and you cry out to Jesus, He will immediately come to your aid! He is *the Soldier of all soldiers* who knows what it feels like to be abandoned in your hour of greatest need (*see* Hebrews 2:18). God may send an angel to strengthen you, or He may impart power to you through His Holy Spirit. Whatever the case, once He touches you, you will have what you need to handle the task in front of you!

God is for you, not against you. He is on your side! He stands ready to give you the divine assistance you need to tackle the assignment He has asked you to do. If you ask Him, He will energize you with His strength so that you can embrace the assignment victoriously. What He did for Jesus, He will do for you!

STUDY QUESTIONS

> **Study to shew thyself approved unto God, a workman that needeth not to be ashamed, rightly dividing the word of truth.**
> **— 2 Timothy 2:15**

1. God's supernatural strength — His *grace* — is available to you. You have His Word on it. Take a few moments to read Isaiah 40:28, 29; James 4:6; and Philippians 4:13. Write out and commit to memory the passage that encourages you most.
2. You may think, *Well, that was Jesus. Surely God would strengthen Him. But how can I know that He will strengthen me?* God answers this question in Deuteronomy 10:17; Romans 2:11; and Acts 10:34, 35. Carefully read these verses and write what He shows you.

PRACTICAL APPLICATION

> **But be ye doers of the word, and not hearers only, deceiving your own selves.**
> **— James 1:22**

1. Jesus knew He needed supernatural strength to submit to and obey the Father's will. He also knew that *prayer* was the channel through which He would receive the power He needed to complete His mission. Briefly describe a tough time in your past when you seriously sought God in prayer and He came through and empowered you to make it through the difficulty.

2. Do you have friends or family members who are going through a stressful situation? What wisdom can you share from this lesson, from God's Word, and from your own relationship with Him that would encourage them in their faith?

LESSON 4

TOPIC
How Many Soldiers Does It Take To Arrest One Man?

SCRIPTURES

1. **John 21:25** —And there are also many other things which Jesus did, the which, if they should be written every one, I suppose that even the world itself could not contain the books that should be written....
2. **John 18:3** — Judas then, having received a band of men and officers from the chief priests and Pharisees, cometh thither with lanterns and torches and weapons.

GREEK WORDS

1. "a band of men" — ϖ (*speira*): a military cohort; a tenth of a legion; approximately 600 soldiers; well-trained soldiers who were equipped with the finest weaponry of the day
2. "officers" — ϖ (*huperetes*): the "police officers" who worked on the temple grounds
3. "a great multitude" of soldiers —   ϖ (*ochlos polus*): a huge or massive multitude (*see* Matthew 26:47)
4. "a great multitude" —   (*ochlos*): a massive crowd (*see* Mark 14:43) and indicated that the band of soldiers who came to the garden was enormous (*see* Luke 22:47)
5. "comprehended" —   μ (*katalambano*): to seize; to grab hold of; to pull down; to tackle; to conquer; to master; to hold under one's power (*see* John 1:5)

SYNOPSIS

Located in the center of the garden of Gethsemane are a number of unique caves. Along with enjoying the peaceful surroundings of the garden, one of these caves was the place Jesus and His disciples regularly visited to rest and pray. Traditionally, it is called the Apostles' Grotto, and it was identified as early as the Fourth Century as the place where Jesus was betrayed.

The emphasis of this lesson:

The night Jesus was arrested in the garden of Gethsemane, the band of soldiers and officers that showed up was not a handful of people as most have believed. It was actually a small army. The legendary power of Jesus was well-known that the enemy prepared accordingly. But the power of darkness was no match for the Messiah — and that same power is available to you today!

After eating the last supper with His disciples, serving them Communion, and washing their feet, Jesus and the 11 men who were with Him made their way toward the garden of Gethsemane. John 18:2 tells us it was Jesus' custom to retire there, and the cave now called the Apostles' Grotto was their specific resting place.

After arriving at the cave, Jesus took Peter, James, and John with Him to another location and asked them to pray. He then went about a stone's throw from them and collapsed under the weight of all that was before Him. Again and again, He cried out to the Father, asking Him to take the cup of suffering away, if it were possible. His will wrestled fiercely against the will of the Father. In the end, Jesus surrendered to God's will and chose to embrace the way of the cross.

When Christ had finished praying and had been supernaturally strengthened by the Father, He returned to the cave where His disciples were resting. Within moments of His return, Judas arrived with soldiers to arrest Jesus and bring Him before Caiaphas and the Jewish council to stand trial.

How Many Soldiers Came To Arrest Jesus?

In Matthew 26:47, we are told that "a great multitude" of soldiers came with Judas. This phrase is taken from the Greek words *ochlos polus*, which describes *a huge or massive multitude*. Similarly, Mark 14:43 also says "a great multitude" with swords accompanied Judas. The phrase "a great multitude" is the Greek word *ochlos*, meaning *a massive crowd*. Once more, in Luke 22:47 it says "a multitude" accompanied the betrayer, which again is the Greek word *ochlos*, indicating that *the band of soldiers who came that night was enormous*.

Just how many soldiers were there? We find the answer in John 18:3. It says, "Judas then, having received *a band of men* and *officers* from the chief priests and Pharisees, cometh thither with lanterns and torches and weapons." The phrase "a band of men" is the Greek military word *speira*. It describes a military *cohort*, which is one-tenth of a legion, or approximately 600 soldiers. These were well-trained fighters who were equipped with the finest weaponry of the day and who reported to the chief priest.

Along with the band of men were "officers" from the chief priests and Pharisees. The term "officers" is the Greek word *huperetes*. These were *the police officers who worked on the temple grounds*. Once an official judgment was given from the religious court, the temple police were responsible to execute the decision. These brutal "officers" worked hand-in-hand with the "band of men" — they assisted the Roman cohort of soldiers.

Where Were the Soldiers From?

The soldiers that Judas Iscariot brought with him were armed forces from the Tower of Antonia. This was a huge facility in the city of Jerusalem that was constructed by Herod the Great. He named it in memory and honor of his friend Mark Antony — the same Mark Antony who was in love with Cleopatra. Interestingly, Herod the Great, Mark Antony, and Cleopatra were all contemporaries of each other.

The military forces stationed in the Tower of Antonia served to counterattack any kind of riot or insurgency that might occur on the temple mount. These were the very soldiers who assisted the temple officers and accompanied Judas Iscariot to the garden of Gethsemane to arrest Jesus.

In the Tower of Antonia, there was a very spacious courtyard large enough to hold a "cohort" of Roman soldiers. Again, a cohort was one-tenth of a legion. Therefore, if a legion of soldiers was 6,000, a cohort would have been 600. That's how many soldiers came with Judas the night he betrayed Jesus — plus the officers who worked on the temple grounds. It was a massive group.

Why Such Large Numbers?

When the cohort of Roman soldiers and the temple police arrived to arrest Jesus that night, the hillside of the Mount of Olives was covered with military troops. While most retellings of this scene depict a half dozen to a dozen soldiers, the truth is it was *hundreds* of armed men. With torches in one hand and weapons in the other, they were prepared to quickly trounce any resistance from Jesus or His disciples.

Normally, it would take anywhere from three to ten men to arrest someone. However, that was not the case with Jesus. Many of the Jewish leaders had personally witnessed His mighty works, and His reputation of supernatural power was also known by the Romans. Therefore, they took no chances. They brought all the forces they could muster in that moment to take Christ into custody.

This also raises the question: What exactly did Judas say to the temple police and the Roman soldiers about Jesus? Did he think Jesus would put up a fight and resist being arrested? Only God knows. Although he had been with Jesus for three years, he apparently didn't really know Him.

Clearly, Christ's power was legendary — even during His own lifetime. John 21:25 says, "And there are also many other things which Jesus did, the which, if they should be written every one, *I suppose* that even the world itself could not contain the books that should be written...." When John said "I suppose," the original Greek means *"it can't be done."*

Jesus had ministered for three years, and miracles occurred everywhere He went. His power was so legendary that His reputation had even reached the ears of Herod Antipas in northern Israel. Luke 23:8 says Herod had longed his entire life to personally see Jesus perform a miracle.

If Herod Antipas, one of the high-ranking ruling authorities in Israel, had heard of Jesus' power, how much more had the soldiers heard? Obviously, they believed it would take a small army to arrest Jesus, so that is what they came with.

That Same Power Is Available to You!

The same supernatural power that operated in Jesus is available to you! The same Holy Spirit who anointed Him is the same Holy Spirit who anoints you. It's no wonder the enemy is terrified of your getting closer to Christ and learning your full identity in Him. He is also afraid of your gathering with other believers and demonstrating the authority and power of Jesus.

In John 14:12, Jesus said, "…He that believeth on me, the works that I do shall he do also; and *greater works* than these shall he do; because I go unto my Father." This means that if Jesus did signs, wonders, and operated in the miraculous, we are to operate in the same way.

Every day, remind yourself of this truth: The same powerfully anointed Spirit that raised Christ from the dead lives in you (*see* Romans 8:11). When thoughts of failure try to attack your mind, recognize they are from the enemy and reject them!

You are a threat to the devil's domain because of the divine power at your disposal. He doesn't have enough power to take you down. John 1:5 confirms this. It says, "And the light shineth in darkness; and the darkness comprehended it not." The word "comprehended" is the Greek term *katalambano*, which means *to seize, to grab hold of, to pull down, to tackle, to conquer, to master, or to hold under one's power*. In other words, the darkness did *not* have the power to take down or master the Light, Jesus Christ! It didn't have the power then, and it doesn't have the power now.

More than 600 armed men came to the cave called the Apostles' Grotto to arrest Jesus. Ironically, no weapons were needed. Jesus didn't resist them. He had already won the war over His will and surrendered to the Father's plan. The Father's will was now completely His will, and His obedience would bring about deliverance and salvation to all who would ever believe in and follow Him.

STUDY QUESTIONS

Study to shew thyself approved unto God, a workman that needeth not to be ashamed, rightly dividing the word of truth.
— 2 Timothy 2:15

1. The facts reveal that *hundreds* of armed soldiers and temple officers came to arrest Jesus — not just a handful of men as most modern retellings depict. How does this knowledge change your understanding of what happened to Jesus the night He was betrayed in Gethsemane?

2. Romans 8:11 declares that the same powerful Holy Spirit that raised Christ from the dead lives in *you*! Carefully read Romans 8:1-16 and identify the blessings of living your life in obedience to the Holy Spirit.

PRACTICAL APPLICATION

> But be ye doers of the word, and not hearers only, deceiving your own selves.
> —James 1:22

1. Of all the miracles and healings Jesus did, what biblical account has the greatest "wow" factor for you? Why is this so amazing to you?
2. The legendary power of Jesus today is demonstrated through His Holy Spirit working in and through our lives. Look back over your life and briefly list (in bulleted form) five or more times when the supernatural power of God showed up to *protect* you, *rescue* you, or *provide* for you. How does remembering these things strengthen your faith?

LESSON 5

TOPIC

Misunderstandings and Suspicions

SCRIPTURES

1. **John 18:3** — Judas then, having received a band of men and officers from the chief priests and Pharisees, cometh thither with lanterns and torches and weapons.
2. **Mark 14:43** — And immediately, while he yet spake, cometh Judas, one of the twelve, and with him a great multitude with swords and staves, from the chief priests and the scribes and the elders.

GREEK WORDS

1. "a band of men" — ϖ (*speira*): a military cohort; a tenth of a legion; approximately 600 soldiers; well-trained soldiers who were equipped with the finest weaponry of the day

2. "officers" — ϖ (*huperetes*): the "police officers" who worked on the temple grounds
3. "a great multitude" (of soldiers) — ϖ (*ochlos polus*): a huge or massive multitude (Matthew 26:47)
4. "a great multitude" — (*ochlos*): a massive crowd (Mark 14:43) and indicated that the band of soldiers who came that night was enormous (Luke 22:47)
5. "lantern" — (*phanos*): a bright and shining light; the equivalent of a First Century flashlight; a light so brilliant that it penetrated darkened areas and revealed things hidden in darkness
6. "torch" — μϖ (*lampas*): a long-burning oil lamp; a lamp that was oil-based, had a long wick, and could burn all night if necessary
7. "weapons" — ϖ (*hoplon*): the full weaponry of a Roman soldier; a belt, a breastplate, greaves, spikes, shoes, an oblong shield, a brass helmet, a sword, and a lance; these were weapons needed for serious combat
8. "sword" — μ (*machaira*): a sword that was an exceptionally brutal weapon; it most often was shorter and shaped like a dagger; a sword used for close-range stabbing; a deadly and frightful weapon that nearly always inflicted a fatal wound
9. "stave" — (*xulon*): a thick, heavy stick made of wood; a heavy-duty, dangerous, hard-hitting club intended to beat someone

SYNOPSIS

The Apostles' Grotto is one of many caves located in the garden of Gethsemane. It is actually the place Jesus and His disciples regularly visited throughout His years of ministry. Its identity as the place where Jesus and the Twelve met was always undisputedly known, but it was *officially* recognized as that place in the Fourth Century. Today it is used as a church. In fact, it has been a church for many centuries. This cave is where Jesus and His disciples went the night He was betrayed. Of course, Judas had accompanied Jesus there on many prior occasions. But on that night, Judas came with a crowd of armed men who had many misunderstandings and suspicions about who Jesus was.

The emphasis of this lesson:

The armed soldiers and temple officers had many misunderstandings and suspicions of who Jesus was — primarily from the things Judas had told them. Based on this misinformation, they armed themselves with lanterns, torches, and weapons. In the end, none of these were needed. Jesus willingly submitted to His captors and walked out the will of the Father.

The Machine of Misinformation

Gossip and the spreading of rumors are extremely dangerous. When one person hears a rumor, he often repeats it to others, who then repeat it to even more people. On and on the story is passed, becoming more twisted and flawed with each subsequent telling. The worst part about misinformation is that what people hear, they usually believe to be true, even when it is not.

Undoubtedly, Judas played a major role in misinforming the soldiers as to who Jesus was and how He would respond. He had seen Jesus perform innumerable miracles and was well-acquainted with supernatural power operating through Him in extraordinary ways. Judas had also been present in the past when religious leaders tried to seize Him, but were unsuccessful. Just when it seemed Jesus was about to be caught or pushed off a cliff to His death, He supernaturally escaped to safety.

When the soldiers and temple police came to arrest Jesus that night in Gethsemane, they were acting on presumptions and rumors about Jesus that were simply not true. Although it is not clear exactly what they heard, it is clear from how they were equipped when they arrived that the stories they had been told must have been really outrageous.

An Accurate Picture of Who Came to Arrest Jesus

John 18:3 says, "Judas then, having received a band of men and officers from the chief priests and Pharisees, cometh thither with lanterns and torches and weapons."

First of all, we see that "a band of men" came with Judas. This phrase is the Greek word *speira*, and it describes a military cohort, which is a tenth of a legion, or approximately 600 well-trained and equipped soldiers. Next, the Bible says "officers" were in the caravan. "Officers" is the Greek word *huperetes*, and it signifies *the police who worked on the temple grounds.* These two groups worked hand in hand and added up to quite a large crowd.

Matthew's, Mark's, and Luke's gospels confirm this. Matthew 26:47 says, "A great multitude" came with Judas. It wasn't five, six, ten, or even twelve soldiers, as we have seen in most movies. It was "a great multitude," which is the Greek phrase *ochlos polus*, meaning *a huge or massive multitude.*

Mark 14:43 also uses the words a "great multitude." This phrase is from the Greek word *ochlos*, which means a *massive crowd.* Then in Luke 22:47, again it says "a multitude" accompanied Judas into the garden. This phrase is from the Greek word *ochlos*, meaning *a massive multitude.* Clearly, the band of soldiers who came that night to arrest Jesus was enormous. This is very different from what most of us have previously imagined. The crowd was at least 600 soldiers in size — *plus* the brutal temple police — and they were all armed to the max.

They Came With *Lanterns*

The first thing John 18:3 tells us they came with is "lanterns." This is the Greek word *phanos*, and it describes *a bright and shining light that was the equivalent of a First Century flashlight.* It was *a light so brilliant that it penetrated darkened areas and revealed things hidden in the darkness.* Although very brilliant in illumination, this type of light was short-lived.

"Lanterns" (*phanos*) were like modern-day floodlights. There were many rocks, caves, tombs, and olive trees with twisted branches in Gethsemane. The soldiers and officers who came obviously thought Jesus and His disciples might scatter and hide themselves. Thus, they brought multiple floodlights to light up every possible hiding place in the garden.

They Came With *Torches*

John also says the soldiers and officers came with "torches." This is the Greek term *lampas*. It is where we get the word *lamp*. It describes *a long-burning oil lamp that was oil-based. It had a long wick and could burn all night if necessary.*

Why would "torches" (*lampas*) have been brought to Gethsemane? Unlike "lanterns" (*phanos*), which were short-lived in duration, "torches" were long-lasting. The soldiers and temple police likely brought these, not knowing how long it would take to find and apprehend Jesus. If it took all night, they were prepared.

So when the cohort of Roman soldiers and the temple officers came into the garden, they had enough lanterns (*phanos*) and torches (*lampas*) to it light up and hunt for Jesus all night if necessary. They were ready to search in every cave and tomb and behind every rock and tree.

They Came With *Weapons*

The Bible says they also came with "weapons." The Greek word for "weapons" is *hoplon*, and it describes *the full weaponry of a Roman soldier: a belt, a breastplate, greaves, spikes, shoes, an oblong shield, a brass helmet, a sword, and a lance*. These were needed for serious combat. The only reason a soldier would carry all these weapons was if he anticipated a fierce confrontation.

Again, this lets us know what was on the minds of the hundreds of soldiers who came to arrest Jesus that night. They were clearly misinformed and suspicious of what might happen. Therefore, they came armed to the max, ready to fight, not knowing exactly how Jesus would demonstrate His supernatural power to perhaps resist them.

Mark's gospel also adds details regarding weaponry. It says, "And immediately, while he yet spake, cometh Judas, one of the twelve, and with him a great multitude with *swords* and *staves*, from the chief priests and the scribes and the elders."

The first weapon mentioned is "swords." The Greek word for "sword" here is *machaira*, which was *an exceptionally brutal weapon*. It was most often *a shorter sword shaped like a dagger that was used for close-range stabbing*. It was *a deadly and frightful weapon that nearly always inflicted a fatal wound*. That is what these hundreds of soldiers and temple police were carrying, which means they were ready to stab and fatally wound whoever got in their way.

Scripture reveals they also had "staves." The word "stave" is from the Greek word *xulon*, and it describes *a thick, heavy stick made of wood*. It was *a heavy-duty, dangerous, hard-hitting club intended to be used to beat someone to death*.

This small army came to arrest Jesus with daggers to draw blood, clubs to beat people, and the full armor of a Roman soldier. Whatever they had been told and whatever they were believing about Him must have been wild and intense. What is most disappointing is that Judas Iscariot was likely the one who fanned the flame of all the rumors they had heard.

Jesus Shattered Their Expectations With Truth

Think about it. Judas Iscariot, the treasurer of Jesus' ministry — the one who worked with Him every day for three years, talking about finances and the budgetary needs of the ministry — really didn't know who Jesus was. Judas had been in constant contact with the Creator of the universe, but he had suspicions and misunderstandings about Him that were not based on truth. The moment he and the armed troops entered the garden, their image of Jesus began to shatter.

Instead of demonstrating His supernatural power and resisting arrest, Jesus willingly surrendered to the soldiers and temple officers. Much to their surprise, He didn't run and hide, nor did He call on legions of angels to come to His rescue. Instead, He yielded to the authority of His captors.

The hundreds of lanterns and torches were not needed. Neither were the swords, the staves, or the Roman armor required for intense confrontations. The time had come for Jesus to fulfill the Father's plan, and that plan included His death, burial, and victorious resurrection.

If you find yourself in a position where you have been misunderstood or people have made false assumptions about who you are, remember what happened to Jesus. Instead of being offended, use the situation as an opportunity to show them who you really are and give God glory. That's what Jesus did, and with His help you can do the same.

STUDY QUESTIONS

Study to shew thyself approved unto God, a workman that needeth not to be ashamed, rightly dividing the word of truth.
— 2 Timothy 2:15

1. In Scripture, gossip is also called evil speech, slander, malice, and guile. (*See* Psalm 34:11-14; Proverbs 17:9; 20:19; 26:20; Ephesians 4:29-31; and 1 Peter 2:1, 2.) What does God really think about such talk? Check out these verses and write what He reveals to you.
2. Just as in the time of the gospels, many people today have mistaken ideas and opinions of who Jesus was. Their perceptions are based on hearsay, media reports, and the traditions of men. Take a few moments

to carefully read Matthew 16:13-17. Then honestly answer the question Jesus asked His disciples in verse 15: "Who do *you* say that I am?"
3. Be honest. What is your perception of who Jesus is based upon?

PRACTICAL APPLICATION

> **But be ye doers of the word, and not hearers only, deceiving your own selves.**
> —James 1:22

1. Jesus was misunderstood by many people, including Judas Iscariot who had been a very close friend to Him for three years. Have you been misunderstood by someone? Is he or she believing something about you that is totally untrue? If so, take a moment to briefly explain the situation.
2. When you learned of the misunderstanding, how did you respond? How do the suspicions and misunderstandings Jesus experienced compared to His response help you see your situation differently? How does it help you respond as He did?
3. If you're in a position where you've been misunderstood or people have made false assumptions about you, remember what happened to Jesus. Pause and pray: "Lord, I don't want to be offended with [*insert person's name*]. Please help me and give me the strength to submit to You. Teach me how to use this situation to show this person who I really am and to give You glory. In Jesus' name." Be still and receive God's strength. Write down anything He speaks to you.

LESSON 6

TOPIC

Kiss of Deception

SCRIPTURES

1. **John 18:3** — Judas then, having received a band of men and officers from the chief priests and Pharisees, cometh thither with lanterns and torches and weapons.

2. **Mark 14:43** — And immediately, while he yet spake, cometh Judas, one of the twelve, and with him a great multitude with swords and staves, from the chief priests and the scribes and the elders.
3. **Matthew 26:14-16** — Then one of the twelve, called Judas Iscariot, went unto the chief priests, and said unto them, What will ye give me, and I will deliver him unto you? And they covenanted with him for thirty pieces of silver. And from that time he sought opportunity to betray him.
4. **Mark 14:44** — And he that betrayed him had given them a token, saying, Whomsoever I shall kiss, that same is he; take him, and lead him away safely.
5. **Matthew 26:50** — And Jesus said unto him, Friend, wherefore art thou come? Then came they, and laid hands on Jesus, and took him.

GREEK WORDS

1. "token" — μ (*sussemon*): a signal previously agreed upon
2. "kiss" — (*phileso*): a word that shows emotion, affection, and love; it was an act or token of deep affection, serious commitment, and covenant shared only between individuals who had a mutual respect for each other or between those who shared a mutual covenant
3. "friend" — (*hetairos*): friend; companion; comrade; can also describe one who poses to be a buddy or confidant, but who in reality has his own interests in mind; one who acts as if he is a genuine and indisputable friend, but actually is acting for self-gain

SYNOPSIS

As we have seen, the garden of Gethsemane at the time of Jesus was very large. It was filled with olive trees, tombs, an orchard, and a number of caves, one of which is known as the Grotto of Gethsemane, or the Apostles' Grotto, the place where Jesus was betrayed. Early historical writers stated that the Apostles' Grotto was the cave where they spent much of their time. We know it was at that place where Judas found Jesus in order to betray Him, offering the Savior the kiss of deception.

The emphasis of this lesson:

Jesus experienced the horrific pain of betrayal at the hands of Judas Iscariot. It was premeditated, deliberate, and well-planned. He had posed

as Jesus' close friend, companion, and confidant, but his focus was self-gain. Interestingly, the signal he arranged with the soldiers to confirm which person to arrest was *a kiss*.

Underground Meetings

Before Judas escorted the armed troops to Gethsemane to arrest Jesus, he had secretly met with the religious leaders to negotiate a deal for arranging Jesus' capture. Matthew 26:14-16 says, "Then one of the twelve, called Judas Iscariot, went unto the chief priests, and said unto them, What will ye give me, and I will deliver him unto you? And they covenanted with him for thirty pieces of silver. And from that time he sought opportunity to betray him."

During those meetings, Judas disclosed information about where and when Jesus and the disciples rested and prayed. This included the cave now referred to as the Apostles' Grotto. Judas also told the officials about Jesus' phenomenal power, which explains why such a large group of soldiers went armed and prepared to arrest Jesus.

Clearly, Judas' betrayal was no accident. It was a deliberate, premeditated, well-planned effort. He had made a covenant with the religious leaders to lead them right to Jesus under the cloak of the night. He had the inside scoop on where Jesus would be and when He would be there. The 30 pieces of silver were in his hand. All he needed to do was find the most opportune time to hand Jesus over. The signal for indicating the one they should arrest would be *a kiss*.

Armed to the Max

John 18:3 says, "Judas then, having received a band of men and officers from the chief priests and Pharisees, cometh thither with lanterns and torches and weapons." We've learned that the phrase "band of men" is the Greek word *speira*, which describes *a Roman cohort or approximately 600 soldiers*. The word "officers" is the Greek word *huperetes*, and it denotes *the police stationed on the temple mount*.

This enormous military force came to Gethsemane to capture Jesus, and they came with lanterns, torches, and weapons. "Lanterns" is the Greek word *phanos*, and it described *a very bright, short-lived floodlight*. "Torches" is the Greek word *lampas*, which were *long-lasting, oil-burning lamps*. And the word "weapons" is the Greek word *hoplon*, which described *the full weaponry of a Roman soldier when he is called into combat.*

The *lanterns* were brought to shine bright, penetrating light into every possible hiding place, and the *torches* were on hand in case the search for Jesus took all night. In addition to the Roman weaponry, Mark 14:43 tells us something else the soldiers and officers carried. It says, "And immediately, while he yet spake, cometh Judas, one of the twelve, and with him a great multitude with swords and staves, from the chief priests and the scribes and the elders." The word "swords" is the Greek word *machaira*, which indicates *a brutal sword shaped like a dagger used for close-range stabbing.* The word "staves" is the Greek word *xulon*, and it describes *a club used for beating someone to death.*

Leading this well-armed but misinformed mob of military troops was Judas Iscariot. Acting on misunderstandings and suspicions, Judas and all who were with him were prepared to hunt for Jesus all night if necessary. They had sufficient lighting and deadly weapons with which to destroy anyone who got in their way.

'Whomsoever I Shall Kiss'

Many of the soldiers who accompanied Judas to arrest Jesus that night had never personally seen Him. Therefore, Judas arranged a special signal to indicate whom they were to capture. Mark 14:44 says, "And he that betrayed him had given them a token, saying, Whomsoever I shall kiss, that same is he; take him, and lead him away safely."

The word "token" is the Greek word *sussemon*, and it describes *a signal previously agreed upon.* The kiss Judas gave Jesus was the signal to let the troops know, "This is the One you need to arrest. Move in swiftly and take Him away."

The word "kiss" here is the Greek term *phileso*. It was used to show *strong emotion, affection, and love.* It was *an act or token of deep affection, serious commitment, and covenant, shared only between individuals who had a mutual respect for each other.* This included husbands and wives and family members. Later, a "kiss" (*phileso*) came to be used as a form of greeting between especially dear and cherished friends. It was not something given to a stranger, which explains Jesus' response to Judas in the garden.

In Matthew 26:50, it says, "And Jesus said unto him, Friend, wherefore art thou come? Then came they, and laid hands on Jesus, and took him." Notice, Jesus didn't say, "Stranger, wherefore art thou come?" He called Judas "friend." This is the Greek word *hetairos*. It indicates *a friend, companion, or comrade*. However, this word can also describe *one who poses as a buddy or confidant, but who in reality has his own interests in mind*. It can picture *one who acts as if he is a genuine and indisputable friend, but actually is acting for self-gain*.

Judas had posed as Jesus' friend, companion, comrade, and confidant. As the treasurer of the ministry, he met with Jesus regularly to discuss financial needs, offerings they received, as well as budgetary items — how and where those funds were to be disbursed. But if Jesus hadn't known it beforehand, the moment Judas showed up in the grotto with hundreds of armed soldiers and temple officers, Jesus knew he was not a friend at all, but a betrayer.

Judas knew he could get away with giving Jesus a kiss on the cheek because he had a covenant relationship with Him. Nevertheless, Judas' kiss was as phony as his fake friendship. He had pretended to be Jesus' pal and confidant, but in reality had been looking out for his own interests the entire time.

When Judas kissed Jesus, it was the equivalent of saying, "You and I are really good friends, Jesus. We're in covenant relationship." Yet it was nothing but a grievous insult — *the kiss of betrayal*. Judas played this game all the way to the end. He remained in the inner circle of Jesus, walking with Him side-by-side all the way to the night he betrayed Him in the garden. Jesus didn't rebuke Judas or put up a fight. He loved him even in the act of his betrayal.

Mixed Signals

Judas had clearly been deceived by the enemy, and he was confused in his understanding of who Jesus was. More than likely, he had told the Jewish leaders and the military troops, "Arm yourselves to the max! This guy is virtually unstoppable. You never know what He's going to do. I've seen Him supernaturally slip away from the crowd, so bring your torches and lanterns just in case we need to search for Him all night. And bring your weapons. You've never confronted power like this!"

Then in his next breath, Judas said, "I'll deliver Jesus to you. All it will take is a kiss. He won't run from me. So the One I walk up to and kiss on the cheek is the One you need to arrest." In Judas' confusion, he sent mixed signals. His thinking was twisted and his reality distorted. That is a perfect picture of a person who is deceived.

Have others betrayed you — people you loved and confided in with whom you were once very close? Like Judas, they were confused and deceived. They didn't know what they were doing. The truth is, those people you loved and trusted were probably never who you thought they were from the beginning. Jesus knows what it feels like to be betrayed, and as you seek Him, He will empower you to handle your own situation in the right way.

STUDY QUESTIONS

> **Study to shew thyself approved unto God, a workman that needeth not to be ashamed, rightly dividing the word of truth.**
> **— 2 Timothy 2:15**

1. Being deceived is a dangerous place to be, and while pride prevents you from seeing your heart's condition, humility opens your eyes to the truth. Read God's wisdom in Jeremiah 17:9 and 10, along with First Samuel 16:7; Proverbs 15:11; 16:2; and 21:2. What insight can you receive and implement from these passages?
2. David understood the truth about our heart and how vital it is to pray and get God involved. Meditate on his prayer in Psalm 139:23 and 24 and make it your own. What is the Lord revealing to you about *your* heart?

PRACTICAL APPLICATION

> **But be ye doers of the word, and not hearers only, deceiving your own selves.**
> **— James 1:22**

1. The Holy Spirit who lives inside you is all-knowing. He yearns to be welcome in every area of your life, including your relationships. If you're open to His counsel, He will alert you to potential danger. Think about it. Has the Holy Spirit been sounding an internal alarm about a person in your life? Have you sensed uneasiness about someone, but ignored it because you wanted to believe the best of that

person? Be still and listen. Who is the Holy Spirit bringing to mind? What actions is He prompting you to take?

2. Judas and the soldiers who were with him acted on misunderstandings and suspicions about Jesus. They did not see Him for who He really was. What are you thinking and believing about Jesus that is inaccurate? Pause and pray: *Holy Spirit, I humble myself before You and ask You to show me any misunderstandings or suspicions I have about Christ that I need to be aware of.* What is the Lord revealing to you?

LESSON 7

TOPIC

Test of Loyalty, Test of Love

SCRIPTURES

1. **Matthew 26:50** — And Jesus said unto him, Friend, wherefore art thou come? Then came they, and laid hands on Jesus, and took him.
2. **Mark 14:44, 45** — And he that betrayed him had given them a token, saying, Whomsoever I shall kiss, that same is he; take him, and lead him away safely. And as soon as he [Judas] was come, he goeth straightway to him, and saith, Master, master; and kissed him.
3. **John 13:13** — Ye call me Master and Lord: and ye say well; for so I am.

GREEK WORDS

1. "friend" — (*hetairos*): friend; companion; comrade; can also describe one who poses to be a buddy or confidante, but who in reality has his own interests in mind; one who acts as if he is a genuine and indisputable friend, but actually is acting for self-gain
2. "kiss" — (*phileso*): depicts not just a kiss of friendship, but a symbol of deep love, affection, obligation, covenant, and relationship; shared only between individuals who had a mutual respect for each other or between those who shared a mutual covenant
3. "master" — (*didaskalos*): a teacher; it is intended to give the idea of one who is a fabulous, masterful teacher; the Greek equivalent for the Hebrew word "rabbi"

4. "Lord" — (*kurios*): one who has ultimate and supreme authority; a supreme master

SYNOPSIS

Gethsemane was a familiar place to Jesus and His disciples, including Judas. It was a place of rest, recreation, and prayer. On the night He was betrayed, Jesus and 11 of His disciples had gone to the cave known as the Apostles' Grotto. It was to this cave that Judas led hundreds of well-armed soldiers to arrest Jesus, the One he called "Teacher."

The emphasis of this lesson:

Judas had a fatal flaw in his character. It had been there from the start. He never actually submitted to Jesus as "Lord" — only as "Teacher." By being open to correction from those in authority, we can guard our hearts against the treacherous trap of pride and deception.

The Critical Moment in Every Relationship

The true level of commitment in every relationship will eventually be tested. A critical moment will arise in which you will discover who you really are and how committed you are to the authority over you. It is the moment of *disagreement* or *conflict*.

It's easy to walk together while you're in agreement. However, when you come to a place where you don't agree and are no longer having an enjoyable time, how you respond is very telling. Will you continue to be in submission to authority? Or will you resist and choose to take matters into your own hands?

The same is true for those under your authority. If you reach a point of disagreement and the person stays and receives your correction, they are truly submitted to your authority. If they reject your correction and leave, they were never truly submitted to your authority.

Judas Iscariot reached a place of disagreement with Jesus about the use of resources. When Mary poured out the very costly ointment on Jesus' feet, Judas became indignant. It was valued at the equivalent of one-year's salary, and Judas argued that it should have been sold and the money given to the poor.

However, Jesus saw the situation differently. He understood that what was happening had prophetic significance. Thus, He responded, "…Let her alone: against the day of my burying hath she kept this. For the poor always ye have with you; but me ye have not always (John 12:7, 8).

In that moment of disagreement, Judas became offended at Jesus. His heart opened to sin, and the devil deposited a seed of betrayal inside him. Judas heard Jesus' words as an arrogant rebuttal instead of a statement of truth. From that moment on, Judas no longer submitted to Jesus' authority and instead took action against Him.

A moment of confrontation is always a moment of revelation. We can say we're in submission to our pastor, our parents, our boss, or our spouse — but the moment will come when we'll find out the truth of whether we are truly in submission. If you have not experienced this yet, you will.

Judas Was a *Fake* Friend

Judas entered the garden of Gethsemane leading the pack of soldiers and temple police and then kissing Jesus on the cheek. If Jesus hadn't known it before, He knew it then — that Judas was a betrayer. Turning to Judas, Jesus said, "…Friend, wherefore art thou come?" (Matthew 26:50)

The word "friend" is the Greek word *hetairos*, which describes *a friend, a companion, or a comrade*. That is what Judas had been. He had served as the treasurer of the ministry, working with Jesus every day for three years. They had talked about the disbursement of funds, paying bills, and feeding the poor. Jesus and Judas Iscariot worked side-by-side for hours, days, and weeks on end. Jesus called him "friend," because that's what Judas had been. He had been a companion, a comrade, and a confidant.

But interestingly, this word "friend" — the Greek word *hetairos* — can also describe *one who poses to be a buddy or confidant, but who in reality has his own interests in mind. It is one who acts as if he is a genuine and indisputable friend but actually is acting for self-gain.*

The moment Judas came into the garden, his true identity was revealed. Although he had pretended to be a genuine and indisputable friend, his real, self-centered nature could no longer be hidden.

Jesus and Judas Were in Covenant

Mark 14:44 says, "He that betrayed him had given them a token, saying, Whomsoever I shall kiss, that same is he; take him, and lead him away safely." The word "kiss" is the Greek word *phileso*, which depicts *not just a kiss of friendship, but a symbol of deep love, affection, obligation, covenant, and relationship.* This pictured *something shared only between individuals who had a mutual respect for each other, or between those who shared a mutual covenant.* By using the word "kiss," we know Jesus and Judas were in covenant relationship.

In the Upper Room during the last supper, Jesus shared Communion with all of His disciples, including Judas. He took the bread, broke it, and everyone ate. Likewise, He took the wine and served it, and everyone drank. The Communion ceremony signified the covenant between Jesus and His disciples.

However, when Judas partook of the bread and the wine, he was only pretending to be in covenant. His actions were a forgery. The reason is, he had just covenanted with the religious leaders for 30 pieces of silver to betray Jesus into their hands (*see* Matthew 26:15). When Judas covenanted with the religious leaders, he broke the original covenant he'd made with Jesus, *or pretended to make,* and brought a curse upon himself.

That is what the apostle Paul was explaining in First Corinthians 11:27. He said, "Wherefore whosoever shall eat this bread, and drink this cup of the Lord, unworthily, shall be guilty of the body and blood of the Lord." The word "unworthily" refers to the condition of the heart. If you don't intend to obey and be faithful to the Lord — if you have betrayal in your heart — you should not partake of Communion.

That's exactly what Judas Iscariot did. He participated in a ceremony of covenant with betrayal in his heart.

Judas' Words Revealed His Heart

Jesus said that out of the overflow of what is in a person's heart, he speaks (*see* Luke 6:45). Judas' heart was revealed by what he said in the garden of Gethsemane. Mark 14:45 says, "And as soon as he [Judas] was come, he goeth straightway to him, and saith, Master, master; and kissed him."

The word "master" in Greek is the word *didaskalos*, which means *a teacher*. It describes *one who is a fabulous, masterful teacher*. It is the Greek equivalent for the Hebrew word *rabbi*. A rabbi was one who was highly respected for his marvelous ability to understand and teach the Scriptures. When Judas said, "Master, master," he was actually saying, "Teacher, masterful teacher!" or "Rabbi, wonderful rabbi!"

This tells us that Judas had only received Jesus and submitted to Him on the level of a teacher or rabbi. He didn't call Him "Lord." In fact, there's no evidence in any of the gospels that he ever called Him "Lord." Judas took the benefits of being with Jesus, but never submitted to His authority.

In John 13:13, Jesus told His disciples, "Ye call me Master and Lord: and ye say well; for so I am." The word "Lord" is the Greek word *kurios*, and it describes *one who has ultimate and supreme authority in one's life; a supreme master*. Jesus was saying, "You call Me Lord (*kurios*), and that is who I am. *I am the supreme authority in your life*." With the exception of Judas, each of the disciples were completely submitted to Christ's authority.

If Judas had really been submitted to Jesus as Lord, he would not have debated with Jesus about how the perfume was used. He would have said, "You are *Lord*. I'm the servant and the student. I don't understand what You're allowing to take place or what You're saying here, but I want to learn. I submit to Your authority."

How about you? What do your words and actions reveal about the position Jesus holds in your life? What about your attitude and actions toward your pastor, government officials, and the other people God has placed over your life? Are you truly submitted to their authority?

STUDY QUESTIONS

> **Study to shew thyself approved unto God, a workman that needeth not to be ashamed, rightly dividing the word of truth.**
> **— 2 Timothy 2:15**

1. According to Romans 13:1 and 2, who has set up a system of authority? When you choose to submit to authority and God's order, what are you actually doing? How about when you resist? (Remember, submission and respect do not equal agreement.)

2. The book of Proverbs has much to say about correction and instruction. Check out these promises and warnings; identify the *blessings* of receiving correction and instruction and the *pain* of rejecting it. (*See* Proverbs 4:1, 13; 8:33, 34; 10:17; 12:1; 15:5, 10; 16:22; and 19:20.)

PRACTICAL APPLICATION

> But be ye doers of the word, and not hearers only,
> deceiving your own selves.
> —James 1:22

1. Generally speaking, how do you react when someone in authority brings you correction? Which types of authority are more difficult for you to receive correction from? Pray and ask the Holy Spirit to reveal to you why this is the case.
2. Be honest. Is Jesus really the *Lord* of your life? Does He have the right to direct and correct *every* area of your life? Is there a specific thing over which you find it difficult to let Him be Lord? If so, what is it? Again, pray and ask the Holy Spirit why this is the case.

LESSON 8

TOPIC

Paralyzed by His Presence

SCRIPTURES

1. **John 18:3-6** — Judas then, having received a band of men and officers from the chief priests and Pharisees, cometh thither with lanterns and torches and weapons. Jesus therefore, knowing all things that should come upon him, went forth, and said unto them, Whom seek ye? They answered him, Jesus of Nazareth. Jesus saith unto them, I am he.... As soon then as he had said unto them, I am he, they went backward, and fell to the ground.
2. **Exodus 3:13, 14** — And Moses said unto God, Behold, when I come unto the children of Israel, and shall say unto them, The God of your fathers hath sent me unto you; and they shall say to me, What is his name? what shall I say unto them? And God said unto Moses, I AM

THAT I AM: and he said, Thus shalt thou say unto the children of Israel, I AM hath sent me unto you.
3. **John 8:58** — Jesus said unto them, Verily, verily, I say unto you, Before Abraham was, I am.

GREEK WORDS

1. "a band of men" — σ (*speira*): a military cohort; a tenth of a legion; approximately 600 soldiers; well-trained soldiers who were equipped with the finest weaponry of the day
2. "officers" — σ (*huperetes*): the "police officers" who worked on the temple grounds
3. "a great multitude" of soldiers — σ (*ochlos polus*): a huge or massive multitude (Matthew 26:47)
4. "a great multitude" — (*ochlos*): a massive crowd (Mark 14:43)
5. "a multitude" — (*ochlos*): indicating that the band of soldiers who came that night was enormous (Luke 22:47)
6. "lantern" — (*phanos*): a bright and shining light; the equivalent of a First Century flashlight; a light so brilliant that it penetrated darkened areas and revealed things hidden in darkness
7. "sword" — μ (*machaira*): a sword that was an exceptionally brutal weapon; it most often was shorter and shaped like a dagger; a sword used for close-range stabbing; a deadly and frightful weapon that nearly always inflicted a fatal wound
8. "stave" — (*xulon*): a thick, heavy stick made of wood; a heavy-duty, dangerous, hard-hitting club intended to beat someone
9. "I am" — μ (*Ego eimi*): "I AM!"
10. "went backward" — σ μ (*aperchomai*): depicts the soldiers and temple police staggering and stumbling backward, as if some force had hit them and was pushing them back and down
11. "fell" — σ σ (*pipto*): to fall; depicts a person who falls so hard that it appears he has fallen dead or has fallen like a corpse
12. "to the ground" — μ (*chamai*): depicts falling abruptly and hitting the ground hard

SYNOPSIS

In the garden of Gethsemane, a supernatural event took place that is often overlooked. Many believers know that Judas' betrayal of Jesus took place in Gethsemane. What many don't know is that it took place in a *cave* in Gethsemane — a cave known as the Apostles' Grotto. Judas led the enormous crowd of soldiers and temple officers there, and they filled the cave, the entrance, and the surrounding hillside. It was inside this cave where Judas approached Jesus and kissed Him. It was also in this cave that the soldiers became *paralyzed by God's presence*.

The emphasis of this lesson:

The soldiers were seeking Jesus of Nazareth. When Jesus answered, *"I am He,"* they were knocked to the ground by a blast of divine power. Christ identified Himself as God, and the supernatural demonstration that made powerful military men *like dead men* validated His claim.

Armed and Dangerous

John 18:3 says, "Judas then, having received a band of men and officers from the chief priests and Pharisees, cometh thither with lanterns and torches and weapons." We've learned that the phrase "band of men'" is the Greek word *speira*, which describes *a military cohort — approximately 600 well-trained soldiers*. The word "officers" is the Greek word *huperetes*, and it describes *the police officers who worked the temple grounds*.

When we add these groups together, it's clear that Judas came with hundreds of armed men — not a handful, which is what has often been depicted in stories about this historical event. In fact, Matthew 26:47 called the group "a great multitude." This is the Greek phrase *ochlos polus*, meaning *a huge or massive multitude*. Mark 14:43 confirms this, also calling the soldiers "a great multitude" — a phrase taken from the Greek word *ochlos*, meaning *a massive crowd*. Even Luke calls the number of soldiers "a multitude" in Luke 22:47. The Greek here also indicates the number of soldiers was enormous.

All of them were carrying "lanterns and torches and weapons." The word "lanterns" is the Greek word *phanos*, which describes *a bright and shining light; the equivalent of a First Century flashlight*. These lanterns were used to penetrate darkened areas and reveal things that were hidden. "Torches" is from the Greek word *lampas*, and it describes *a long-burning, oil-based oil lamp with a long wick.* These lamps could burn all night if necessary. The combination of hundreds of lanterns and torches meant that the soldiers brought enough light to illuminate the entire garden of Gethsemane all night long.

They also had "weapons," which is the Greek word *hoplon*. This describes *the full weaponry of a Roman soldier: the belt, the breastplate, the greaves, the spikes, the shoes, the shield, the helmet, the sword, and the lance.* These weapons were intended for serious combat.

And according to Mark 14:43, the armed men also came with "swords and staves." "Swords" is the Greek word *machaira*, which was *an exceptionally brutal sword. It was often shorter and shaped like a dagger; it was used for close-range stabbing.* The word "staves" is the Greek word *xulon*, which describes *a thick, heavy wooden stick. It was a dangerous, heavy-duty, hard-hitting club often used to beat people to death.*

This is the picture of the massive crowd of Roman soldiers and temple police led by Judas Iscariot that night! Hundreds of men carrying lanterns, torches, and weapons, including lethal swords and staves, descended on the Apostles' Grotto in Gethsemane. They were ready for an all-out war.

Jesus Identified Himself as 'I AM'

The story continues in John 18:4 and 5: "Jesus therefore, knowing all things that should come upon him, went forth, and said unto them, Whom seek ye? They answered him, Jesus of Nazareth. Jesus saith unto them, I am he. And Judas also, which betrayed him, stood with them."

When the guards said they were looking for Jesus of Nazareth, notice Jesus' reply: *"I am He."* This phrase "I am" is the Greek phrase *Ego eimi*, which simply means *I am*. On the surface, this may seem like nothing special. However, a closer look at the words *Ego eimi* in the light of Scripture reveals that these are the same words God used to identify Himself to Moses in Exodus 3:13 and 14.

> And Moses said unto God, Behold, when I come unto the children of Israel, and shall say unto them, The God of your fathers hath sent me unto you; and they shall say to me, What is his name? what shall I say unto them? And God said unto Moses, I AM THAT I AM: and he said, Thus shalt thou say unto the children of Israel, I AM hath sent me unto you.

The phrase "I AM" that God used in Exodus 3:14 is *the same one* Jesus used in John 18:5 — the Greek words *Ego eimi*. This is confirmed in the Septuagint, which is the Greek translation of the Old Testament.

When Jesus Christ told the soldiers "I am he," He was telling them, "I AM GOD." He was literally identifying Himself as the God of the Old Testament.

This wasn't the first time Jesus identified Himself as God. In John 8:58, "Jesus said unto them, Verily, verily, I say unto you, Before Abraham was, *I am*." Here again, the words "I am" are the Greek phrase *Ego eimi*.

In John 13:19, Jesus said, "Now I tell you before it come, that, when it is come to pass, ye may believe that I am he." Again, when Jesus said "I am he," it is the Greek phrase, "*Ego eimi*." He identified Himself as the God of the Old Testament.

They Fell as if They Were Dead

What happened when Jesus answered "I AM" is astounding. In John 18:6, it says, "As soon then as he had said unto them, I am he, they went backward, and fell to the ground." The phrase "went backward" is the Greek word *aperchomai*, which depicts the soldiers and temple police *staggering and stumbling backward, as if some force had hit them and was pushing them back and down*.

Not only does the Scripture say they "went backward," it also says they "fell to the ground." The word "fell" is the Greek word *pipto*, which means *to fall*. However, this isn't an ordinary fall. This fall depicts *a person who falls so hard that it appears he has fallen dead or has fallen like a corpse*. And the phrase "to the ground" is the Greek word *chamai*, which depicts *falling abruptly and hitting the ground hard*.

When Jesus answered and said, "I am" (*Ego eimi*), there was a blast of supernatural power released. It hit the hundreds of soldiers and temple police that were present, causing them to stumble, stagger, and eventually fall to the ground as if they were dead. It was like an invisible "bomb" had been detonated the instant Jesus uttered the words "I AM," causing everyone present to fall down hard, completely involuntarily and unexpectedly.

Imagine that. Military men armed to the max, ready for a fight to the finish, knocked to the ground by the power of Jesus Christ! What a shock that must have been. Instead of just rumors and stories about the power of

Jesus, they now had a firsthand experience with His power that surpassed their wildest imaginations.

Once Jesus clearly demonstrated He could not be taken by force, He willingly surrendered Himself. He knew it was the will of the Father for Him to go to the cross and become "the Lamb of God that takes away the sin of the world" (*see* John 1:29).

Speak the Word of God

Jesus was and still is the Great I AM! When He spoke the Word of God, supernatural power of God was detonated. As a believer, you are in Christ. You have been given the Word of God. And you have the ability and the authority to speak His Word over yourself, your situation, and the enemy's schemes.

The power of God that was available to Jesus is available to you. When the enemy comes against you and says, "I'm going to take you down," you need to open your mouth and speak the Word from your heart. When you do, divine power will be released to lay the enemy flat on his face.

STUDY QUESTIONS

> **Study to shew thyself approved unto God, a workman that needeth not to be ashamed, rightly dividing the word of truth.**
> **— 2 Timothy 2:15**

1. One of the greatest verses of Scripture revealing the power of God's Word is Hebrews 4:12. Look up this passage in a few different translations. Write it out in the version that speaks to you most powerfully.
2. Proverbs 18:21 declares, "Death and life are in the power of the tongue…." The words you speak pack power. Take a moment to meditate on the words of Jeremiah 23:28, 29. What is the Holy Spirit telling you through this passage?

PRACTICAL APPLICATION

> But be ye doers of the word, and not hearers only, deceiving your own selves.
> —James 1:22

1. Again and again, Jesus identified Himself as the "Great I AM" — which is how He also identified Himself in the Old Testament. What

does that name speak to you of God's timelessness and eternal presence? What does that presence means to your life right now?
2. In the garden of Gethsemane, Jesus was surrounded by His enemies. Yet when He spoke the words "I AM," they were brought to the ground. Stop and think — what is the greatest enemy coming against you? Using a Bible concordance or an online search engine, find at least *three scriptures* that you can commit to memory and speak out over your life. The enemy is no match for God's divine power.

LESSON 9

TOPIC

The Danger of Taking Matters Into Your Own Hands

SCRIPTURES

1. **Luke 22:49** — When they which were about him saw what would follow, they said unto him, Lord, shall we smite with the sword?
2. **John 18:10** — Then Simon Peter having a sword drew it, and smote the high priest's servant, and cut off his right ear. The servant's name was Malchus.

GREEK WORDS

1. "smite" — ϖ   (*patasso*): to strike with intent to kill
2. "smote" — ϖ   (*paio*): to strike, as a person who viciously strikes someone with a dangerous tool, weapon, or instrument; can also be translated to sting like a scorpion that injects its stinger into a victim; to beat with the fist; in this verse, it pictures the force of Peter's swinging action
3. "cut off" — ϖ ϖ (*apokopto*): pictures a downward swing that cuts something off; to castrate
4. "ear" —   (*otaion*): refers to the entire outer ear
5. "Malchus" —   (*Malchos*): ruler and counselor

SYNOPSIS

Today the Apostles' Grotto in the garden of Gethsemane is used as a church. In fact, it has been a church for many centuries. Early history states that many events recorded in Scripture actually took place in this cave. For instance, it was here that Judas came with hundreds of armed men and kissed Jesus, betraying Him into enemy hands. It was also the place where Jesus spoke the words, *"I Am He,"* and hundreds of soldiers were knocked to the ground, paralyzed by the power of God. It was also in this cave where Peter let his emotions get the best of him, and he impetuously took matters into his own hands.

The emphasis of this lesson:

When the going got tough, Peter took matters into his own hands, recklessly attacking the servant of the high priest, cutting off his ear. Hotheaded moments rarely produce good fruit. But Jesus will often clean up our mess if we cry out penitently to Him for help.

Scenes of Gethsemane in Jesus' Final Hours

Jesus Experienced Agony: In Luke 22:44, we saw Jesus in "agony"— the Greek word *agonia*, which describes *two men in a wrestling match*. Jesus was in a wrestling match: His will wrestled against the will of God. The agony was *an intense competition, battle, and exertion*.

Jesus' struggle was so passionate that He prayed to the Father three times saying, "If it be possible, let this cup pass from me: nevertheless not as I will, but as thou wilt" (Matthew 26:39). The internal fight was so fierce that He sweat great drops of blood (*see* Luke 22:44). Finally, after being strengthened by God through an angel, Jesus fully surrendered and embraced the Father's will.

Know that if you're going through a difficult time, God will provide divine assistance for you.

Judas Iscariot Arrived: Just as Jesus got up from praying and winning the battle in the Spirit, Judas appeared on the scene with "a band of men" (*see* John 18:3). The phrase "band of men" is the Greek word *speira*, and it described *a Roman cohort, which was one-tenth of a legion, or 600 soldiers.* There were also numerous temple officers with him, making the crowd that came to arrest Jesus enormous.

Jesus' power was legendary, and they had all heard of it. Apparently, Judas believed Jesus would demonstrate supernatural power to resist His arrest. What exactly he told the religious leaders and soldiers is unknown. But what he said must have filled their minds with misunderstandings and suspicions.

Soldiers Came With Weapons: The word "weapons" is the Greek word *hoplon*, and it means *the full weaponry of a Roman soldier who is outfitted for a serious combat*. The men also came with "swords and staves" (*see* Mark 14:43). "Swords" is the Greek word *machaira*, which was *an exceptionally brutal dagger-shaped sword for close-range stabbing*. The word "staves" is the Greek word *xulon*, which describes *heavy-duty clubs used to beat someone to death*. These soldiers were equipped for a fight to the finish.

Soldiers Came With Lanterns and Torches: With brightly shining lanterns to illuminate dark places and oil-burning torches that were long-lasting, these armed troops were ready to search for Jesus, all night if necessary.

Remember, Jesus had supernaturally disappeared from His enemies on more than one occasion. Judas Iscariot had been there each time. More than likely, Judas told the soldiers, "You better come ready. Bring lanterns and torches. It could take all night. This Man can slip away in an instant." Thus, they came prepared to search and fight until they captured Jesus.

Judas Calls Jesus "Master" and "Teacher": Although Jesus and Judas had worked together every day for years, Judas didn't know intimately who Jesus was. Judas was deceived and confused. Jesus wasn't going to fight those soldiers, nor was He going to run from the call of God on His life. But Judas didn't know this because he had been allowing things into his heart that caused his relationship with Christ to be flawed from the beginning.

The night Judas betrayed Jesus, he came to Him and addressed Him as "Master." The word "master" is the Greek word *didaskalos*, which means *masterful teacher*. It is the Greek equivalent of *rabbi*. When Judas addressed Jesus as "Master, master," he was literally saying, "Masterful teacher, masterful teacher." He didn't call Jesus "Lord." In fact, there's no evidence anywhere in the gospels that Judas ever called Jesus Lord.

The word "Lord" is the Greek word *kurios*, and it means *someone who has ultimate and supreme authority and control in one's life*. When someone is *kurios* in our lives, he or she is the one we fully obey. Judas didn't use this title. He had only received Jesus as a masterful teacher. Although he received the benefits of Jesus' teaching and enjoyed living in the orbit of His spectacular ministry, Judas never fully submitted to Jesus' lordship. This was revealed by his words that fateful night. Seized with satanic deception, Judas called Jesus "Master" and "Teacher." Then he betrayed Jesus with a kiss.

Jesus Identified and Powerfully Demonstrated Himself as God: Turning to the soldiers, Jesus asked, "Whom do you seek?" After they answered, "Jesus of Nazareth," they probably expected Him to say, "I'm Jesus of Nazareth." Instead, He said, *"I Am He."* The phrase "I Am" is the Greek phrase *Ego eimi* — the same words God used in Exodus 3:14 to identify Himself to Moses as "the Great I AM." By saying, "I Am," Jesus was identifying Himself as the God of the Old Testament in the flesh.

Amazingly, the moment Jesus spoke the words "I Am," John 18:6 says the soldiers "went backward, and fell to the ground." The phrase "went backward" is the Greek word *aperchomai*, which indicates the soldiers *stumbled, trying in vain to resist the power that was pressing them backward and downward.* But the power was so strong, they *couldn't* resist it, and the Bible says they "fell to the ground." The word "fell" is the Greek word *pipto*, which means *to fall hard like a corpse.* The word "ground" is the Greek word *chamai*, which means *they fell and smacked the ground really hard.*

Peter Swings Into Action, Taking Matters Into His Own Hands

Knocked flat to the ground by a blast of divine power, the soldiers lay there paralyzed. Knowing the enemy's intent and seeing the opportunity before him, Peter immediately moved into action. Luke 22:49 says, "When they which were about him saw what would follow, they said unto him, Lord, shall we smite with the sword?"

The word "smite" is the Greek word *patasso*, which means *to strike with the intention of killing.* Peter, being rash and impetuous in his thoughts and actions, took a sword and intended to kill the person he hit. Was the sword Peter's? It's not certain. Some scholars believe Peter saw the soldiers knocked to the ground by the power of the Holy Spirit, and he reached down and picked up one of their swords.

John 18:10 says, "Then Simon Peter having a sword drew it, and smote the high priest's servant, and cut off his right ear. The servant's name was Malchus." The word "smote" is the Greek word *paio*, which means *to strike,* as a person who viciously strikes someone with a dangerous tool, weapon, or instrument. It can also be translated *to sting, like a scorpion that injects its stinger into a victim or to beat with the fist.* In this verse, it pictures *the full force of Peter's swinging action.*

Who Was Malchus? Why Smite Him?

Clearly, Peter viciously struck Malchus with all his might and intended to kill him. But who was Malchus? Did Peter randomly choose to attack him or was his selected victim strategic? Malchus was a high-level servant. Specifically, he was the high priest's spokesman. Caiaphas served as the high priest, and whenever he had something to say, he said it through his spokesman Malchus. When Caiaphas voiced slanderous and blasphemous accusations against Jesus, Malchus was usually the one to speak them publicly. Every attack, every venomous statement he uttered, was delivered throughout Israel by the mouth of Malchus.

Caiaphas was a Sadducee, and Sadducees didn't believe in the supernatural. Every supernatural, Old Testament event was considered a myth and legend. Like the beliefs of many mainline denominational people today, supernatural activity was simply explained away. Therefore, when Jesus came along displaying miraculous signs and wonders, they disliked Him instantly. Caiaphas took every opportunity to discredit Jesus, but when he did, he did it through his public-relations man Malchus.

Obviously, Peter knew who Malchus was. Seeing him brought back painful memories. From Peter's perspective, Malchus represented everything he disliked about the religious community. When he saw Malchus paralyzed on the ground by the power of God, he saw an irresistible opportunity to strike down one of Jesus' most vocal enemies. More than likely, Peter acted out of an angry, bitter grudge in his heart toward Malchus.

The word "Malchus" in Greek is *Malchos,* meaning *ruler or counselor.* Whether this was actually his name or simply a title given to him, we know he was a man of prominence. As a public spokesman of the high priest, he was very well-known. By modern standards he would have been regarded as a celebrity, and for Peter to strike a celebrity was a very serious offense.

Cut Off Completely, But Restored by the Lord

Some have said that Peter just nipped the ear of Malchus, but that is not what the original text reveals. John 18:10 says that Peter "...cut off his right ear." The phrase "cut off" is the Greek word *apokopto*, and it describes *a hard, downward swing that cuts something completely off*. It's the same word that can be translated *to castrate*. The word "ear" is the Greek word *otaion*, and it refers to *the entire outer ear*.

When Peter swung that sword, he likely intended to decapitate Malchus, but he was only successful at cutting off his ear. Had Peter been a soldier and not a fisherman, he probably would have severed Malchus' head, but instead he cut off his ear clear to the bone.

Did Jesus ask for or need Peter's help? No. He was God in the flesh. With the utterance of two words, He flattened His foes to the ground — hundreds of them — in one fell swoop. As a result of Peter's reckless actions and taking matters into his own hands, Jesus would need to step up and clean up Peter's mess.

STUDY QUESTIONS

> Study to shew thyself approved unto God, a workman that needeth not to be ashamed, rightly dividing the word of truth.
> — 2 Timothy 2:15

1. Recklessly taking action without thinking can cause very undesirable consequences. Consider what God says in these verses about being hasty. What wisdom can you gain and apply in your life from these truths? (*See* Proverbs 19:2; 21:5; 29:20; James 1:19, 20; and Acts 19:36.)
2. One of the most valuable virtues the Holy Spirit produces in our lives is self-control. Check out these related scriptures and write a brief prayer asking the Lord to develop the fruit of self-control in you. (*See* Proverbs 16:32; 25:28; Galatians 5:22, 23; and 2 Peter 1:3-8.)

PRACTICAL APPLICATION

> But be ye doers of the word, and not hearers only, deceiving your own selves.
> — James 1:22

1. Can you think of a time when you became so impatient that you could no longer wait on the Lord to act, so you took matters into your

own hands? Briefly describe what happened. If you knew then what you know now, how would you have acted differently in that moment?
2. Acting recklessly in the heat of the moment rarely produces anything good. What words of wisdom and caution would you share with a dear friend who is on the verge of taking matters into his or her own hands?

LESSON 10

TOPIC

Jesus Cleans Up Peter's Mess

SCRIPTURES

1. **Luke 22:51** — And Jesus answered and said, Suffer ye thus far. And he touched his ear, and healed him.
2. **John 18:10** — Then Simon Peter having a sword drew it, and smote the high priest's servant, and cut off his right ear. The servant's name was Malchus.

GREEK WORDS

1. "touched" — ϖ μ (*haptomai*): to firmly grasp or hold tightly; to aggressively touch
2. "healed" — μ (*iaomai*): to cure, restore, or heal

SYNOPSIS

Most of what happened in the garden of Gethsemane took place in the Apostles' Grotto — a cave recognized in the Fourth Century as the place where Judas Iscariot betrayed Jesus. The grotto is also the place where Peter acted impetuously, cutting off the ear of Malchus, the servant of the high priest. Without thought of what his actions would bring, Peter made a mess of things. But Jesus didn't leave him to fend for himself. Instead, He immediately stepped in and cleaned up his mess.

The emphasis of this lesson:

Many times we make a mess of things completely on our own. That's what Peter did in the garden. Knowing Peter couldn't fix what he had broken, Jesus stepped in and straightened out what Peter messed up. He offers us the same help if we'll cry out to Him in faith.

As we have seen, Judas led a band of hundreds of soldiers and temple police to the garden of Gethsemane the night he betrayed Jesus. They were heavily armed and had enough lighting to illuminate the entire hillside throughout the night as they sought for Jesus to take Him into custody.

John 18:4 and 5 says, "Jesus therefore, knowing all things that should come upon him, went forth, and said unto them, Whom seek ye? They answered him, Jesus of Nazareth. Jesus saith unto them, I am he...."

The phrase "I am" is the Greek phrase *Ego eimi*. These are the same words God used in Exodus 3:14 when He identified himself to Moses as "I AM THAT I AM." By using the words *Ego eimi* (I am), Jesus was identifying Himself as God in the flesh.

John 18:6 goes on to say, "As soon then as he had said unto them, I am he, they went backward, and fell to the ground." Jesus' words detonated so much spiritual power that the soldiers could no longer stand on their feet, but were knocked to the ground. There they were — hundreds of soldiers and temple officers — incapacitated by the power of God. And among them was a man named Malchus.

Malchus Was Caiaphas' Mouthpiece

Malchus was the servant of the high priest Caiaphas. He was his public spokesman. Caiaphas was the leader of the Sadducees who didn't believe in supernatural occurrences. They dismissed all the miraculous events of the Old Testament as being myths or legends. They didn't believe in or embrace the idea of anything supernatural, including the resurrection.

Jesus' entire ministry brought the miraculous to life. And since the Sadducees hated the supernatural, they hated Jesus and all for which He stood. Again, Caiaphas was the leader of the Sadducees, and Malchus was his spokesman. Whenever Caiaphas had something venomous to say about Jesus, he didn't say it himself publicly, because that wasn't politically smart.

Instead, he would voice his slander and accusations through his mouthpiece Malchus.

In that moment, when Peter saw Malchus lying on the ground in the midst of the paralyzed soldiers, a flood of bad memories undoubtedly came crashing to his mind. All the vile things Malchus had said and spread about Jesus, His ministry, and His disciples — all the lies, the insinuations, and the rumors he spoke on behalf of Caiaphas had not been forgotten. A fiery rage fueled by a long-held grudge pushed Peter over the edge. He probably thought, *This is my opportunity!*

Peter Acted Rashly

John 18:10 says, "Then Simon Peter having a sword drew it, and smote the high priest's servant, and cut off his right ear...." The word "smote" is the Greek word *paio*, which means *to strike as a person who is viciously striking someone else*. In other words, Peter swung hard and viciously at Malchus. The word "smote" can also be translated *to sting, like a scorpion that injects its stinger into a victim, or to beat with the fist*. In this verse, it pictures *the full force of Peter's swinging action*.

The scripture goes on to say Peter "cut off" Malchus' right ear. This phrase "cut off" is the Greek word *apokopto*, which describes *a downward swing that cuts something completely off*. It can also be translated *to castrate*. Clearly, Peter didn't just nip Malchus' ear; he severed it to the bone. He completely removed the ear from Malchus' head!

This was a very serious crime. Some suggest that Peter took the sword of one of the Roman soldiers, which was a criminal offense in itself. However he obtained the sword, Peter then attacked a well-known official — one who held the status of a celebrity. These serious infractions would have led to Peter's arrest. He would have been charged for his crimes, imprisoned, and possibly executed. His impetuous actions would have destroyed his marriage, his family, his ministry, and his life. Clearly, he was in deep trouble.

Imagine the Situation From Jesus' Perspective

Jesus had been in intense agony — His own will was wrestling against the will of the Father. The internal conflict was so severe He began sweating great drops of blood. After being strengthened by an angel sent from God, He was finally able to surrender His will to the will of the Father and embrace the cross and all that was before Him.

Upon returning to the cave where His disciples were resting, Jesus was met by Judas Iscariot and about 600 hundred armed men who accompanied him. Betrayed by a kiss, Jesus asked the mob who they were looking for, and they answered, "Jesus of Nazareth." When He replied, *"I Am He,"* the soldiers were knocked to the ground by a blast of divine power.

As the men lay there motionless on the ground, Peter saw an opportunity to strike back at his enemies. Grabbing a sword, he swung it and cut off the ear of Malchus, the high priest's servant.

There stood Jesus — watching all this play out before His eyes. He knew the Scriptures and everything He was about to face. Jesus knew He would stand trial before the religious leaders and before Pilate. He knew He would be scourged and receive the stripes that would provide our healing. He also knew He would be crucified and suffer hellish torment. All this and more weighed heavily upon His mind. But now, in the midst of it all, Peter had recklessly taken matters into his own hands, creating a bloody mess by severing Malchus' ear.

Jesus Intervened

Interestingly, Jesus didn't tell Peter, "You made this mess on your own, so it's up to you to clean it up." He also didn't berate him and say, "What's the matter with you, Peter? What were you thinking, flying off the handle like that? Don't you know what I'm dealing with here?" On the contrary, Jesus, the Good Shepherd, stepped in and quietly began to clean up Peter's mess.

Luke 22:51 says, "And Jesus answered and said, Suffer ye thus far. And he touched his ear, and healed him."

Jesus' statement, "Suffer ye thus far," could better be translated, "Let Me just do one more thing before you take Me." It was as if He pressed *pause* on everything and said, "Give Me a minute…I need to take care of some business," and then He fixed the mess Peter created by his rash actions.

Scripture says Jesus "…touched his ear, and healed him." The word "touched" is the Greek word *haptomai*, which means *to firmly grasp, to hold tightly* or *to aggressively touch*. This word gives us insight as to how Jesus prayed for the sick. He didn't just gently lay hands on Malchus. He probably placed both hands on him and began to aggressively pray. Onlookers would have likely seen Malchus' head shaking in the hands of Jesus as He firmly grasped him.

Not only did Jesus touch Malchus, He also "healed" him. The word "healed" is the Greek word *iaomai*, which in this particular verse means *to cure, to restore,* or *to heal.* The Bible doesn't tell us if Jesus prayed and Malchus grew a new ear or if Jesus picked up the ear that had been cut off and "knitted" it back to Malchus' head. Nevertheless, one of these two things happened.

But why? Why take the time to stop and heal a person who viciously spewed venomous words against Him? Why did Jesus not just go into custody with the soldiers and leave Peter to clean up his own mess? First, Jesus is a Healer and He always heals. Second, Jesus didn't want Peter to be arrested for his impulsive actions. By healing Malchus, Jesus delivered Peter from his mess.

Had Jesus not intervened, Peter's life would have been destroyed. His actions kept Peter from being arrested, going to trial and prison, and possibly being executed. He saved Peter's marriage, his family, and his ministry. Peter went on to become the leading apostle of the Church. None of what God had planned for Peter would have taken place had Jesus not intervened.

You're Not Too Busy

Have you ever made a mess of things in your life? Have you said or done things in haste that you deeply regretted later? You're not alone. Thankfully, God is always ready and willing to step in and graciously clean up our mess if we will humble ourselves and ask Him for help.

And the next time you think *you're* too busy to stop and intervene on someone's behalf, remember Jesus. The night He was betrayed and on the way to His trial, scourging, and crucifixion, He took time to help Peter by cleaning up his mess. If you see that someone has made a mess of things in his life, do what you can to help him clean it up. It's what Jesus did, and it's what He does today.

STUDY QUESTIONS

Study to shew thyself approved unto God, a workman that needeth not to be ashamed, rightly dividing the word of truth.
— 2 Timothy 2:15

1. After Peter made a mess of things, he was a bruised and broken man. Yet even in the midst of Peter's brokenness, Jesus reached out in love and restored him — which is exactly what He wants to do for us. Regardless of what you've done or how you feel, Jesus is waiting with arms open wide for you. What has He promised to do for those who are broken? Find out in Psalm 34:17, 18; 147:3; Isaiah 66:2; and Matthew 12:20.
2. Peter couldn't stand the sight of Malchus. His heart was filled with bitterness that had gone unchecked. Do you find yourself in this situation with someone in your life, whose face or name ignites a rage within you? Read Mark 11:25, 26; Ephesians 4:31, 32; and First Peter 3:8, 9. Then pray: Lord, please forgive me for holding unforgiveness toward [insert person's name]. I release _____ into Your hands. Just as You have forgiven and blessed me, I choose, with Your help and strength, to forgive and bless _____.

PRACTICAL APPLICATION

> But be ye doers of the word, and not hearers only,
> deceiving your own selves.
> —James 1:22

1. Look back over your life. Can you remember a time when you acted recklessly and it created a huge mess? How did God step into your situation and clean things up? What specific people or provision did He place there to help you?
2. Like Peter, have you had trouble forgiving yourself for that mistake? If so, Jesus stands ready, willing, and able to help. Take a moment to pray, receive His forgiveness, and ask for His wisdom and grace to move forward.
3. Has anyone in your inner circle (friends or family) recently found himself in a situation similar to yours? How can you reach out to help him move toward Jesus?

LESSON 11

TOPIC
Twelve Legions of Angels

SCRIPTURES
1. **Matthew 26:53** — Thinkest thou that I cannot now pray to my Father, and he shall presently give me more than twelve legions of angels?
2. **John 19:11** — Jesus answered, Thou couldest have no power at all against me, except it were given thee from above: therefore he that delivereth me unto thee hath the greater sin.

GREEK WORDS
1. "legion" — *(legeon)*: a military term taken from the Roman army that denoted approximately 6,000 Roman soldiers

SYNOPSIS
As we have seen, the garden of Gethsemane at the time of Jesus was very large. It contained an orchard of trees, many graves, and multiple caves. These caves became known as the Grottos of Gethsemane, and ancient sources tell us that one of them was where Jesus and His disciples frequently retreated for rest and fellowship. This was where He went the night He was betrayed. Judas was very familiar with the place, and He knew Jesus would be there that eventful night. Along with a band of approximately 600 military men and temple police, Judas went there and betrayed Jesus with a kiss. Yet even in the midst of being betrayed, Christ's power manifested mightily.

The emphasis of this lesson:

The night Jesus was arrested in Gethsemane, He revealed that He had 12 legions of angels available to assist Him at any moment. Their combined strength was more than enough to wipe out all of mankind. Nevertheless, Jesus didn't call on them. He knew the Father's will was for Him to go to Calvary. Therefore, He willingly submitted to God's plan.

One Cave, Many Events

In the previous lessons, we have learned about many amazing events that took place in the cave in Gethsemane called the Apostles' Grotto.

Jesus said, "I am." Upon their arrival, Jesus asked the soldiers, "…Whom seek ye? They answered him, Jesus of Nazareth. Jesus saith unto them, I am he…" (John 18:4, 5). The phrase "I am" is the Greek phrase *Ego eimi* — the same words God used in Exodus 3:14 when He revealed His identity to Moses as "I AM THAT I AM."

By responding "I am," *Ego eimi,* Jesus was identifying Himself as the God of the Old Testament in the flesh. The instant He uttered "I am," John 18:6 says the soldiers "went backward, and fell to the ground." A blast of divine power knocked them flat on their backs. In the Greek, the word "fell" is *pipto,* meaning *to fall so hard that it appears one has fallen dead like a corpse.* And the word "ground" is the Greek word *chamai,* which indicates *they smacked the earth very hard.*

Peter swung into action. While the armed troops lay on the ground, paralyzed by God's power, Peter took matters into his own hands. John 18:10 says, "Then Simon Peter having a sword drew it, and smote the high priest's servant, and cut off his right ear. The servant's name was Malchus."

We have learned that the word "smote" is the Greek word *paio,* which means *to strike, as a person who viciously strikes someone.* It can also be translated *to sting, like a scorpion that injects its stinger into a victim,* or *to beat with the fist.* In this verse, it pictures *the full force of Peter's swinging action.* With all his might, Peter swung and "cut off" Malchus' ear. "Cut off" is the Greek word *apokopto,* and it describes *a downward swing that cuts something off completely.* It is the same word that can be translated *to castrate.* Peter completely severed Malchus' ear from his skull.

Malchus was in the line of fire. Caiaphas was the high priest at that time, and Malchus was his public spokesman. He was a well-known, high-level official with a celebrity status. Whenever Caiaphas wanted to say something vicious or slanderous about Jesus and His disciples publicly, he was politically correct and said it through his spokesman Malchus.

Again and again, Peter had heard Malchus maliciously attack Jesus and the disciples. Hence, Peter had no doubt developed a bitter grudge, and finally released his anger against his enemy. When Peter saw Malchus lying on the ground incapacitated by the power of God, he had his opportunity to take revenge.

Jesus cleaned up Peter's mess. Clearly, Peter could have been arrested and tried for his actions. More than likely, his deed would have resulted in imprisonment or possibly execution. What he had done to Malchus was a criminal offense.

Jesus never asked for Peter's help. Peter acted completely on his own accord. Yet instead of telling Peter, "You made the mess, so you deal with it," Jesus intervened. Luke 22:51 says that as they were arresting Jesus, "Jesus answered and said, Suffer ye thus far," which was like saying, "Before you take Me, let Me do just one more thing." The verse goes on to say, "And he *touched* his [Malchus'] ear, and healed him."

"Touched" is the Greek word *haptomai*, which means *to firmly grasp, to hold tightly*, or *to aggressively touch*. Jesus firmly laid His hands on Malchus' bleeding head. More than likely, there was a whole lot of shaking going on! Whether Jesus grew a new ear for Malchus or picked up the ear that Peter had cut off and knitted it back to Malchus' head, the Bible doesn't say. Nonetheless, Jesus did one of those two things and "healed" him. "Healed" is the Greek word *iaomai*, which means *to cure, to restore*, or *to heal*. When Jesus removed His hands from Malchus, his ear was completely restored.

Much power was on display in Gethsemane. Hundreds of soldiers were knocked to the ground by the words of Jesus. A man's ear, which had been severed from his head, was fully restored. And Peter escaped being arrested, imprisoned, and possibly executed as a result of Jesus' miraculous intervention.

What Is a Legion?

Having just miraculously healed Malchus' ear, Jesus told Peter to put away his sword. He then turned to the soldiers and said, "Thinkest thou that I cannot now pray to my Father, and he shall presently give me more than twelve legions of angels?" (Matthew 26:53).

Jesus said the Father would "presently give" Him angelic protection. This means that *immediately, in that very moment*, God would have dispatched angels on Christ's behalf. How many angels were available to Jesus? He said "more than twelve legions."

The word "legion" is the Greek word *legeon*. It is *a military term taken from the Roman army that denoted approximately 6,000 Roman soldiers*. Every time you hear or see the word "legion" in Scripture, you can always know it is referring to approximately 6,000 in number. For example, in Mark 5:9 Jesus encountered a man living among the tombs who was possessed with a "legion" of evil spirits. That means there were about 6,000 demons controlling this man. But Jesus cast them all out and set the man free!

How Many Angels Are in Twelve Legions?

Jesus said He had "more than twelve legions of angels" available to Him *instantly, in that present moment*. Since a legion of angels is at least 6,000, 12 legions would be 12 multiplied by 6,000. That's 72,000 angels that were on standby ready to help the Master. At any moment, Jesus could have prayed to the Father, and He would have dispatched all those angels to assist Jesus in whatever way He needed.

Interestingly, at the beginning of Jesus' life, there was a multitude of angels present at His birth (*see* Luke 2:13, 14). They filled the sky and gave God glory and praise for His miraculous incarnation. Angels were also present throughout Jesus' ministry, and at the end of His life, a multitude of angels were on call to assist Him — all He had to do was say the word.

What Was the Combined Power of Twelve Legions?

Angels are extremely powerful beings. The Bible records an account in Isaiah 37:36 in which one angel killed 185,000 men in the enemy's camp. Since one angel could destroy 185,000, the combined strength in a legion of angels, which is 6,000, could wipe out 1,110,000,000 men (that is, *1 billion, 110 million* men) — and that's just the combined power of *one* legion of angels!

Since one legion of angels can destroy *1 billion, 110 million men*, how many men can 12 legions of angels kill? By doing the math, we see 72,000 angels multiplied by 185,000 equals *13,320,000,000* men! Therefore, the combined strength of 12 legions of angels (72,000 angels) that were at Jesus' disposal was enough to destroy at least *13 billion, 320 million* men — which is about twice the population of the earth today at the time of this publication.

The soldiers and religious leaders didn't have the power to out-muscle the Master. When Pilate told Jesus, "…Knowest thou not that I have the power to crucify thee, and have the power to release thee? Jesus answered, Thou couldest have no power at all against me, except it were given thee from above…" (John 19:10, 11). Thus, Jesus' life was not forcibly taken; He willingly laid it down.

Clearly, Jesus didn't need Peter's sword to protect Him. He already had everything needed to defend Himself. All He had to do was say the word, and the angels would have rushed to His aid. Yet Jesus refrained from calling on them. He knew it was the Father's plan for Him to die on the cross and take away the sin of the world. Therefore, like a sheep before the shearers, He opened not His mouth — He silently submitted and surrendered Himself to God's will.

Learn a Lesson From Peter

Peter's reckless actions are a perfect example of what *not* to do. He showed us how the flesh tries to solve its problems, but it cannot. Jesus didn't ask for Peter's help, and unless God asks you to do something, don't take matters into your own hands. He is well able to handle any situation in your life — whether it's a situation with your marriage, your children, your job, your finances, or your health.

Before you fly off the handle and say or do something you will later regret, stop and pray. Say, "Lord, what are You doing in this situation? Is it Your will for me do what I am about to do? Or is it Your will for me to be still and yield to what's happening as I trust You?"

Listen to what God says. If He asks you to do something, do it. Yet always remember to let God be God. He can handle anything that comes your way.

STUDY QUESTIONS

> Study to shew thyself approved unto God, a workman that needeth not to be ashamed, rightly dividing the word of truth.
> — 2 Timothy 2:15

1. Angels are real and very powerful. From Genesis to Revelation, they enter and exit earth's scene, carrying out God's special assignments. According to Psalm 91:11, 12 and Hebrews 1:14, what are two primary jobs that angels carry out?

2. Taking matters into your own hands can be deadly. How effective can you expect to be when you do things in your own strength? Read Psalm 127:1; John 6:63; 15:5; and Romans 7:18 for the eye-opening answer.

PRACTICAL APPLICATION

> But be ye doers of the word, and not hearers only, deceiving your own selves.
> —James 1:22

1. By healing Malchus, Jesus destroyed any incriminating evidence against Peter, effectively freeing him from the consequences of his actions. He has done the same for us! What mistakes in your life are you especially grateful Jesus took care of for you?
2. Jesus declared He was able to call on angels at any moment to come to His assistance and defend Him. Since "…as he is, so are we in this world" (*see* 1 John 4:17), we have that same ability. How does this knowledge boost your confidence in God's ability to protect you?

LESSON 12

TOPIC

Who Is the Naked Boy in the Garden of Gethsemane?

SCRIPTURES

1. **Mark 14:51, 52** — And there followed him [Jesus] a certain young man, having a linen cloth cast about his naked body; and the young men laid hold on him: and he left the linen cloth, and fled from them naked. (*Other uses of linen cloth:* Matthew 27:59, Mark 15:46, and Luke 23:53.)
2. **John 19:11** — …Thou couldest have no power at all against me [Jesus], except it were given thee from above….

GREEK WORDS

1. "linen cloth" — (*sindon*): used in the New Testament only to depict a linen cloth in which individuals were wrapped for burial; thus, a burial shroud used for covering a dead body in the grave. The only usage we have for this kind of cloth in the New Testament is that of a burial shroud used for covering a dead body in the grave
2. "followed" — (*sunakoloutheo*): to follow; to continuously follow

SYNOPSIS

Gethsemane was quite an immense place in Jesus' day. It covered nearly the entire slope of the Mount of Olives. Although we call it the garden of Gethsemane, it contained much more than just a grove of olive trees. As we have seen, it had multiple caves, which became known as the Grottos of Gethsemane, as well as a cemetery with many graves. This cemetery would play a major role in the miracle that took place as recorded in Mark 14:51 and 52.

The emphasis of this lesson:

In addition to the soldiers being knocked to the ground by a blast of divine power and the miraculous restoration of Malchus' severed ear, there was another supernatural event that took place on this fateful night. It is seen in the life of the young man who was dressed in only a linen cloth — a boy who was brought back to life by Jesus' resurrection power!

When the temple police and cohort of Roman soldiers, about 600 in number, came to arrest Jesus in the Apostles' Grotto, He asked them, "Whom seek ye?" They answered, "Jesus of Nazareth," and Jesus replied, *"I am he"* (*see* John 18:4, 5).

When Jesus said, "I am," the Greek words *Ego eimi*, He was using the same words God used to identify Himself to Moses in Exodus 3:14. This means He identified Himself as God in the flesh, and the moment He did, a blast of divine power was released, knocking the soldiers and temple officers backward and down to the ground.

Dazed, stunned, and temporarily incapacitated, the armed men struggled to regain their bearings. Meanwhile, Peter's eye caught the sight of Malchus, the high priest's servant, on the ground nearby. Without thinking, he grabbed a sword and swung viciously at the servant, cutting off his right ear. Jesus reached out and firmly grasped Malchus' head and totally restored his ear.

Angels Waiting in the Wings

At that point, Jesus turned to the soldiers and declared, "Thinkest thou that I cannot now pray to my Father, and he shall presently give me more than twelve legions of angels?" (Matthew 26:53). The words "presently give" indicate the idea of *right now, at this very moment*. All Jesus needed to do was say the word, and the Father would have sent more than 12 legions of angels to assist Him.

We saw in the last lesson that the word "legion" is the Greek word *legeon*, and it is *a military term taken from the Roman army that denoted about 6,000 Roman soldiers*. In fact, every time you see the word "legion," it describes something that is 6,000 in number. Thus, one legion of angels would be 6,000 angels. Twelve legions of angels would be 6,000 multiplied by 12, which equals 72,000 angels.

What is the combined strength of 72,000 angels? Isaiah 37:36 tells us that just one angel killed 185,000 men who were coming against the people of Israel. If one angel destroyed 185,000 men, and one *legion of angels* is 6,000, then one legion of angels could potentially destroy 1,110,000,000 people.

But Jesus didn't have just one legion of angels (6,000) at His disposal — *He had more than 12 legions!*

That means there were at least 72,000 angels waiting in the wings to come to Christ's rescue the moment He gave the word. Since one angel can destroy 185,000 people (*see* Isaiah 37:36), 72,000 angels can wipe out 13,320,000,000 people! That number is almost twice the population of the earth today!

Interestingly, during the time Jesus was on earth, there were approximately 60 million people in the Roman Empire. This means there were enough angels to destroy the population of the entire empire. This was the invisible army readily available at Jesus' command. However, He didn't call on them. He knew it was His Father's will for Him to surrender Himself peacefully and be crucified, and that is what He did.

Uncovering the Identity of the Naked Boy

Immediately after all these events, Mark 14:51 and 52 describes something an event that was quite out of the ordinary. It says, "And there followed him a certain young man, having a linen cloth cast about his naked body; and the young men laid hold on him: and he left the linen cloth, and fled from them naked."

A number of scholars have explained that the young man who was naked in Gethsemane was Mark himself. They claim that for some unknown reason, he suddenly appeared in the garden without any clothes. However, this makes no sense and doesn't fit within the context of the passage. Others have stated that the young man naked in the garden was the apostle John. They speculate that when Jesus was being arrested, John attempted to create a diversion by removing his clothes to distract the soldiers. This too is an outlandish notion that doesn't fit within the context of what took place.

To know the true identity of the naked boy in Gethsemane that night, we must dig deeper into the original Greek used in this passage.

The garden of Gethsemane was not only spread out to encompass an orchard and multiple caves, but it also had a cemetery at its base. This means that there were many graves in the garden, and a number of them would have been freshly carved in rock for people who had just been buried.

This brings us to two key words in Mark 14:51 and 52. It says the young man had a "...*linen cloth* cast about his naked body..." (Mark 14:51). The rest of that passage says, "...The young men laid hold on him: And he left the *linen cloth*, and fled from them naked."

The words "linen cloth" is the Greek word *sindon*. The only usage of this word in the New Testament was to depict a linen cloth in which individuals were wrapped for burial. Thus, it was *a burial shroud used for covering a dead body in the grave.*

When Jews prepared a body for burial, they ceremonially cleansed and purified it. The naked corpse was then carefully wrapped with a "linen cloth" — a burial shroud — and placed in a grave. The Greek word *sindon* ("linen cloth") is the exact same word used to describe Jesus' own burial shroud in Matthew 27:59; Mark 15:46; and Luke 23:53.

Apparently, a young man had recently died. His body had been ceremonially cleaned, wrapped in a fresh linen cloth, and placed in a grave. When Jesus answered the soldiers and said, "I am," declaring that He was God in the flesh, the same supernatural blast of power that knocked them backward and to the ground evidently touched this recently buried young man, and raised him from the dead! That is why he was dressed with only a "linen cloth" or *a burial shroud.*

Therefore, the naked boy in the garden of Gethsemane was a young man who had been raised from the dead. This was peripheral resurrection; it was not directly intentional. The power released through Jesus was just that strong!

Nothing But *Power, Power, Power* on Display!

Imagine the scene. As Jesus willingly submitted to the soldiers, allowing them to arrest Him, a young man who had been recently buried was raised from the dead. Mark 14:51 says, "And there followed him a certain young man, having a linen cloth…." The word "followed" is the Greek term *sunakoloutheo*, which means *to follow continuously.* This tells us the young man was trailing the soldiers for some time, probably trying to catch a glimpse of the One who had brought him back to life.

Suddenly, the members of the mob taking Jesus into custody saw this young man carrying his burial shroud. Realizing he had been raised from the dead, they tried to seize him. The last thing the soldiers and religious leaders wanted at that moment was news of yet another miracle at the hands of Jesus. Nevertheless, their attempts failed, and the young man escaped naked, leaving his burial shroud in their hands.

There they were — more than 600 Roman soldiers and temple police. They had just regained their bearings after being knocked to the ground by a divine blast of Jesus' power. They had also just witnessed Malchus, the high priest's servant, have his ear cut off and then miraculously restored by Jesus. Furthermore, Jesus had just informed them of the 12 legions of angels standing by to assist Him at His call. Now they were seeing a young man come back to life, racing away from them naked! There was nothing but *power, power, power* on display in that garden!

Jesus' power is extraordinary! Even in the most difficult hours of His life, He was demonstrating His divine ability. And through His Holy Spirit, He is still releasing His anointing today. If you will reach out in faith, the same power that was seen in Gethsemane will be released in *your* life to accomplish all kinds of amazing things!

STUDY QUESTIONS

> Study to shew thyself approved unto God, a workman that needeth not to be ashamed, rightly dividing the word of truth.
> — 2 Timothy 2:15

1. Prior to these lessons, how have you viewed the events that took place in the garden of Gethsemane? In what ways have these lessons enriched and expanded your perspective?
2. How does knowing that a young man was raised from the dead transform your understanding of Mark 14:51 and 52? What surprised you most about this story? (Also consider the details and events surrounding the prophet Elisha's tomb in 2 Kings 13:20, 21.)

PRACTICAL APPLICATION

> But be ye doers of the word, and not hearers only, deceiving your own selves.
> — James 1:22

1. What circumstances are you presently experiencing in which you need Jesus to say, *"I am,"* and release His divine power on your behalf? Pray and invite the Holy Spirit into your situation.
2. After seeing the power of Jesus displayed right before their eyes, the temple officers and soldiers still refused to declare and submit to the lordship of Jesus. Are there areas in your life that you have not submitted to Jesus' lordship? If so, which ones? Take a moment to ask Him to forgive you and then to surrender those areas to Him.

LESSON 13

TOPIC
Has Anyone Ever Spit in Your Face?

SCRIPTURES
1. **Matthew 26:67-68** — Then did they spit in his face, and buffeted him; and others smote him with the palms of their hands, saying, Prophesy unto us, thou Christ, Who is he that smote thee?
2. **John 1:11** — He came unto his own, and his own received him not.

GREEK WORDS
1. "spit" — μω (*emptuo*): to spit; to spit in someone's face was the strongest act one could take to show utter disgust, repugnance, dislike, or hatred; to spatter spit on another person's face was meant to humiliate, demean, debase, and shame that person; to make it worse, the offender would usually spit hard and close to the person's face, making it all the more humiliating
2. "buffet" — (*kolaphidzo*): to strike with the fist; usually pictures a person who is violently beaten
3. "smote" — ω (*rhapidzo*): to strike with the palm of the hand; to slap

SYNOPSIS
In the city of Jerusalem, the Tower of Antonia once stood. It was a magnificent military fortress built by Herod the Great in honor of his friend, Mark Antony. Antony was the lover of Cleopatra and a contemporary of Herod three or four decades before the time of Christ. It was to this tower that Jesus was taken the night He was betrayed. Pilate's palace was located there. It was the place where Jesus would be judged and sentenced to death.

The emphasis of this lesson:

The cruelty and humiliation Jesus endured by approximately 100 abusers before He was even tried, convicted, and hanged on the cross was

more than anyone should have to suffer. But Jesus refused to be removed from the path of God's will, which would lead Him all the way to Calvary. Covered with saliva from being spit on, and bruised from being beaten and slapped by the sadistic hands of His captors, Jesus would not be deterred. Although He could have called 12 legions of angels to rescue Him even then, Jesus had become one with the will of the Father to redeem mankind from Satan's hellish grip. The joy of fulfilling His assignment for you and me sustained Him amidst the shame.

No one on earth — individually or collectively — had enough power or authority to arrest Jesus and lead Him away to be tortured and crucified. He could have called upon 12 legions of angels to come to His aid and stop the whole attack in an instant. *But He didn't.* Jesus knew that the horrors He would suffer were actually the Father's plan to redeem humanity and regain the relationship with man that Adam and Eve forfeited in the garden of Eden. So Jesus willingly yielded to the sadistic whims of His captors.

An Amazing Chain of Events

In the last several lessons, we saw that Christ's power was demonstrated mightily in the Apostles' Grotto in the garden of Gethsemane. When Jesus identified Himself to the soldiers with the words *"I am,"* divine power was "detonated." It was so strong and explosive that the temple police and the cohort of soldiers — about 600 in number — fell hard to the ground, as if they were dead.

In that moment, Peter grabbed a sword and swung it at Malchus, the high priest's spokesman, cutting off his right ear. Moments later, Jesus firmly placed His hands on Malchus and spectacularly healed that injury, fully restoring his ear. Jesus then alerted His arresters that He could summon 12 legions of angels to come to His aid. But He didn't call for backup! Instead, He submitted Himself to the soldiers, knowing it was God's will that He suffer and die for the sins of mankind.

As the armed troops began to make their way out of the cave and through the garden with Jesus, a naked boy wearing nothing but a linen cloth — a burial shroud — began to follow the mob. Apparently, when Jesus spoke the words, "I am," the power that was released in that moment raised this young man back to life. Crawling out of his grave with his burial cloth, the young man followed Jesus and the crowd as closely as possible. But when the soldiers tried to catch him, he quickly slipped through their hands and escaped.

They *Spit* in His Face

Mark 14:53 says, "And they led Jesus away to the high priest; and with him were assembled all the chief priests and the elders and the scribes." The first place where Jesus was led was Caiaphas' palace, where He stood before the scribes and elders. After several attempts at interrogating Jesus and drumming up false witnesses to testify against Him, Matthew 26:67, 68 says, "Then did they spit in his face, and buffeted him; and others smote him with the palms of their hands, saying, Prophesy unto us, thou Christ, Who is he that smote thee?"

It says, "Then did they spit in his face…." The word "spit" is the Greek word *emptuo*, which means *to spatter spit upon*. In that culture and time, if you wanted to show total repugnance for someone, you would gather as much saliva as you could in your mouth and then get right up in a person's face and spit as hard as you could. To spatter spit on another person's face was meant to humiliate, demean, debase, and shame that person. This was the strongest act a person could perform to show total disgust, dislike, or even hatred for someone.

That night, scholars estimate Jesus was sitting in the palace of Caiaphas with about 100 religious leaders. One by one, they stood in front of Him, taking turns spitting in His face as hard as they could. By the time they were finished, Jesus's hair, face, beard, and clothing were literally dripping with the spit of those religious leaders. Outwardly, those men looked so dignified with their ornate religious robes. But inwardly they were rotten, and they passionately hated Jesus.

They *Buffeted* Him

Not only did the religious leaders spit in Jesus' face, they also "buffeted Him." The word "buffet" is the well-known Greek word *kolaphidzo*, which means *to strike with the fist*. It usually pictures a person who is violently beaten. The religious leaders clenched their fists and began striking Jesus in the head, the face, and anywhere they could.

Remember, there was about 100 men at Caiaphas' palace, all having equal opportunity to punch Jesus with their fists with all their might. The fact that Scripture says "they" spat on Him and "they" buffeted Him lets us know many, if not all, of them took turns humiliating and beating Jesus. This was not only brutal, but twisted, sick, and sadistic. It was an all-out demonic attack.

Others *Smote* Him

Once they got tired of spitting on and buffeting Jesus, Matthew 26:67 says, "…Others smote Him with the palms of their hands." The word "smote" is the Greek word *rhapidzo*, and it means *to strike with the palm of the hand or to slap*. Again, a line formed and people took turns slapping Jesus in the face.

While they spit on Him, repeatedly beat Him with their fists, and slapped Him with the palms of their hands, then they began to play games with Him, "Saying, Prophesy unto us, thou Christ, Who is he that smote thee?" (Matthew 26:68). Mark's and Luke's accounts say they "blindfolded Him" (*see* Mark 14:65; Luke 22:64). The word "blindfolded" in the Greek means *they put a wrapping around His face so that He couldn't see what was happening to Him or around Him*.

Malchus Was Among Them

Knowing all this was taking place at the high priest's palace, more than likely the servant of the high priest was present. In other words, in the midst of all the spitting, punching, and slapping they were doing to Jesus, Malchus was there.

Remember, Malchus was in the garden of Gethsemane with the armed soldiers, overseeing the capture of Christ. He was the one who had his ear cut off by Peter and then was miraculously healed by Jesus. Malchus would have helped lead the procession to Caiaphas' palace that night for the mock trial. And it's very possible that Malchus got caught up in the moment and participated in all the spitting, beating, and slapping that was done to Jesus.

Operating With a Perverted Passion

These religious leaders hated Jesus passionately, and a large number of them were Sadducees. Remember, the Sadducees didn't believe in or want anything to do with the supernatural. They explained away all the miraculous stories of the Old Testament as superstitious legends and myths.

Jesus represented everything they despised. His ministry was all about the miraculous. He was the Messiah — the Anointed One of God. When they spit on Jesus, they were spitting on the anointing. When they beat Jesus with their fists, they were beating the anointing. When they slapped Jesus with the palms of their hands, they were slapping the anointing. The religious leaders despised the anointing of God operating through Jesus' life, and by attacking Him, they attacked the anointing.

John 1:11 says, "He came unto his own, and his own received him not." These were Jesus' own, and they treated Him dreadfully. What might have happened had the people of Israel been allowed to peek into the room that night? How might they have responded and what might they have thought of their "dignified and spiritual" religious leaders?

Like a Lamb to the Slaughter

Matthew 27:1 and 2 record, "When the morning was come, all the chief priests and elders of the people took counsel against Jesus to put him to death: and when they had bound him, they led him away, and delivered him to Pontius Pilate the governor."

Notice it says, "…They led Him…." The word "led" is from the Greek word *ago*, which is the same word used to describe *tying a rope around the neck of a lamb and leading it somewhere*. Isaiah 53:7 speaks of Jesus, saying, "…He is brought as a lamb to the slaughter…."

No one on earth had enough power or authority to arrest Jesus and lead Him away to suffer the cruelty and abused the Savior endured. He could have called upon 12 legions of angels to come to His aid and stop the whole event. *But He didn't.* Jesus knew this was the Father's plan, so He simply yielded to the whims of His captors.

STUDY QUESTIONS

> Study to shew thyself approved unto God, a workman that needeth not to be ashamed, rightly dividing the word of truth.
> — 2 Timothy 2:15

1. Have you been severely mistreated or abused? Jesus knows how you feel. First, take a moment to look up Hebrews 2:14-18 and 4:15, 16.

Then, take time to go to the Lord in prayer and pour out your heart. He will listen, He will heal you, and He will show you what to do.
2. Hebrews 13:3 (*NLT*) says, "Remember those in prison, as if you were there yourself. Remember also those being mistreated, as if you felt their pain in your own bodies." In what practical ways might this scripture be lived out in your life right now?

PRACTICAL APPLICATION

> But be ye doers of the word, and not hearers only,
> deceiving your own selves.
> —James 1:22

1. Have you ever felt like someone "spit in your face?" In what ways can you personally identify with the story Rick shared about a church that publicly ridiculed, lied about, and acted maliciously toward him and his church?
2. The Holy Spirit asked Rick to "sow a seed for peace" into the same church that had treated him and his church so dreadfully. Is the Holy Spirit asking you to sow a seed for peace into the life of the person who has severely mistreated you? If so, explain what He's asking you to do.
3. Clearly, it was Jesus' own will and nothing else that kept Him submitted to the Father's will to die in our place on Calvary. How does this realization expand your understanding of the depth and purity of God's love for you?

LESSON 14

TOPIC

Playing Games at Jesus' Expense

SCRIPTURES

1. **Luke 22:63-65** — And the men that held Jesus mocked him, and smote him. And when they had blindfolded him, they struck him on the face, and asked him, saying, Prophesy, who is it that smote thee? And many other things blasphemously spake they against him.

2. **Matthew 23:27** — Woe unto you, scribes and Pharisees, hypocrites! for ye are like unto whited sepulchres, which indeed appear beautiful outward, but are within full of dead men's bones, and of all uncleanness.
3. **1 Peter 2:21, 22** — For even hereunto were ye called: because Christ also suffered for us, leaving us an example, that ye should follow his steps: who did no sin, neither was guile found in his mouth.

GREEK WORDS

1. "mock" — μω (*empaidzo*): to play a game; often used for playing a game with children or for amusing a crowd by impersonating someone in a silly and exaggerated way; this word might be used in a game of charades when someone intends to comically portray someone else or even make fun of, ridicule, or mock someone; to impersonate someone in a silly and exaggerated way
2. "smote" — (*dero*): the grueling and barbaric practice of beating a slave; a word so dreadful that it is also translated *to flay*, such as to flay the flesh from an animal or human being; to flog; to scourge
3. "blindfolded" — ω ω (*perikalupto*): to wrap a veil or garment about someone, thus hiding his eyes so he can't see; pictures one who is blindfolded; to cover, to wrap around; to hide one's eyes
4. "struck" — ω (*paio*): to strike, as a person who viciously strikes someone with a dangerous tool, weapon, or instrument; can also be translated *to sting*, like a scorpion that injects its stinger into a victim; to beat with the fist
5. "blasphemously" — μ (*blasphemeo*): to speak derogatory words for the purpose of injuring or harming one's reputation; depicts profane, foul, unclean language; in general, any derogatory speech intended to defame, injure, or harm another's reputation; includes any type of debasing, derogatory, nasty, shameful, or ugly speech or behavior intended to humiliate someone

SYNOPSIS

Mark Antony, Cleopatra, and Herod the Great were all contemporaries living in the same era of history. To honor and memorialize his friend Antony, Herod built the Tower of Antonia — a military fortress located in the northeast corner of the Temple Mount in Jerusalem. Years later, it became the palace of Pontius Pilate. It was the base of operation for the temple officers as well as a cohort of Roman soldiers. The night Jesus was arrested in Gethsemane, He was first brought to this tower where He was severely mistreated by the temple police.

The emphasis of this lesson:

After His arrest in the garden of Gethsemane and before Jesus stood before Caiaphas and the religious leaders, Jesus underwent barbaric abuse at the hands of the temple police. They mocked Him, smote Him, and played games at His expense — impersonating Him blasphemously and beating Him violently.

As we saw in our last lesson, Jesus was led from the garden of Gethsemane to be taken to Caiaphas' palace. But before He reached the palace, Jesus' captors made a stop at the Tower of Antonia, where He suffered humiliating abuse, as we will see later in this lesson.

Abuse in the Garden, the Tower, and the Palace

In review, Caiaphas was the high priest and a Sadducee — a sect of religious leaders that didn't believe in the resurrection and wanted nothing to do with supernatural occurrences. They explained away the miraculous events of the Old Testament as purely superstitious legends and myths. Therefore, Jesus was the epitome of everything they despised. So when they finally got their hands on Him, they struck out against Him vehemently.

Matthew 26:67 and 68 says, "Then did they spit in his face, and buffeted him; and others smote him with the palms of their hands, saying, Prophesy unto us, thou Christ, Who is he that smote thee?" Most scholars believe there were about a hundred religious leaders present at this gathering, and the Scripture says, "Then did they spit in his face...."

The word "spit" is the Greek word which generally means *to spit* or *to spatter spit upon*. But to spit *in someone's face* was the ultimate act of utter disgust, repugnance, dislike, or hatred. To spit in a person's face was meant to humiliate, demean, debase and shame someone. The offender would gather as much saliva in their mouth as they could, get right in front of the person he despised, and spit as forcefully as possible in that person's face. This is what those approximately 100 priests and scribes did to Jesus in the palace of Caiaphas. By the time they were finished spitting on Jesus, He had spit dripping from His hair, His face, His beard, and all over His clothes. It was a humiliating, disgusting experience.

From there, the abuse intensified. Next, Scripture says they "buffeted" Him. "Buffeted" is the Greek word *kolaphidzo*, which means *to double-up the fist and strike as hard as one can*. Usually, this pictures *a person who is violently beaten*. Again, the religious leaders took turns beating Jesus with their fists. One after another they struck Him with all their might in His head and face.

Matthew 26:67 goes on to say they "…smote him with the palms of their hands." The word "smote" is the Greek word *rhapidzo*, which means *to slap*. After they had spit on Jesus in utter contempt and pummeled Him with their fists, they began slapping Him across the face. All the while, they chided Him, "Saying, Prophesy unto us, thou Christ, Who is he that smote thee?" (v. 68).

As noted previously, Malchus, the high priest's servant, was likely present and therefore probably participated in the brutality ranged against Jesus. He had overseen the events in Gethsemane, and in the process, had his ear cut off by Peter. Moments later, his ear was completely healed, making him the final recipient of a miracle in Jesus' earthly ministry. Yet in spite of all Jesus had done for Malchus, he likely got caught up in the heat of the riotous rage and joined in the abuse.

Sadly, this was not the beginning of Christ's abuse after His dramatic arrest in Gethsemane. The first round of assaults began in the Tower of Antonia at the hands of the brutal temple police.

Abused in the Tower of Antonia

Before Jesus endured the physical and verbal assaults of the scribes and priests, He was met with equally violent treatment from members of the mob that had arrested Him in the garden of Gethsemane. Specifically, the temple police were the first group to abuse Him. They, too, had heard of Jesus' prophetic healing ministry, so they wanted to put Him to the test. Luke 22:63 tells us, "And the men that held Jesus mocked him, and smote him."

First, they "mocked" Him. The word "mocked" is the Greek word *empaidzo*, which means *to play a game*. Often this word was used for *playing a game with children or for amusing a crowd by impersonating someone in a silly and exaggerated way*. This word might be used in a game of charades when someone intends to comically portray someone or even to make fun of, ridicule, or mock someone. It indicates *impersonating someone in a silly and exaggerated way*.

The soldiers guarding Jesus played games with Him at His expense. More than likely, they took turns impersonating Jesus, pretending to heal people and deliver them from demons. Likewise, they probably pretended to be someone who was healed — acting as though their blinded eyes had been opened or their crippled legs were suddenly healed and they could walk. It was a game of charades in which Jesus was made the laughingstock of every scene.

Then they "smote" Him. The word "smote" is the Greek word *dero*. It describes *the grueling and barbaric practice of beating a slave*. This word is so dreadful that it is also translated *to flay*, such as *to flay the flesh from an animal or human being*. It can also mean *to flog* or *to scourge*. The temple police literally beat Jesus like one would have beaten a slave.

They also blindfolded Him. After being mocked and smote, Luke 22:64 says, "And when they had blindfolded him, they struck him on the face, and asked him, saying, Prophesy, who is it that smote thee?" The word "blindfolded" is the Greek word *perikalupto*, which means *to wrap a veil or garment about someone, thus hiding his eyes so he can't see*. It pictures *one who is blindfolded*. The temple police took a garment of some kind and completely wrapped it around Jesus' head.

Then they "struck" Him. The word "struck" is from the Greek word *paio*, meaning *to strike, as a person who viciously strikes someone with a dangerous tool, weapon, or instrument*. It can also be translated *to sting, like a scorpion that injects its stinger into a victim* or *to beat with the fist*. By using the word *paio*, it denotes that they were beating Jesus with their fists as well as some kind of weapon or instrument.

Again, Jesus was blindfolded through this pummeling. With each hit, the officers would sadistically sneer and say things like, "Prophesy, Jesus. Tell us who just hit You. If You're really a prophet, name the one who just slapped You." Again and again, person after person viciously struck and smote the Lord. It was a terribly grueling experience.

They blasphemed Him. Luke 22:65 reveals, "And many other things blasphemously spake they against him." The word "blasphemously" is from the Greek word *blasphemeo*, which means *to speak derogatory words for the purpose of injuring or harming one's reputation*. It describes *profane, foul, unclean language*. In general, it conveys *any derogatory speech intended to defame, injure, or harm another's reputation*. It includes *any type of debasing, derogatory, nasty, shameful, or ugly speech or behavior intended to humiliate someone*.

The temple police were rough, crude military men. They were stationed at the Tower of Antonia on the Temple Mount to crush any kind of uprising or insurgency. You can imagine how foul they were as they screamed their insults uncontrollably at Christ. It was the human expression of a demonically induced force unleashed on the Son of God.

Again, Jesus experienced all of these hideous brutalities *before* He was delivered to Caiaphas and the religious leaders. He endured this abuse in addition to the intense cruelty from the scribes and Pharisees. Modern movies usually lump all the beatings and mockery into one session, but that is historically inaccurate. The physical violence Jesus bore was lengthy, repeated, and occurred on multiple occasions before He finally made His way to Calvary on Golgotha's hill.

Jesus Is Our Example

Without question, Jesus went through a great deal for us — a horrific ordeal. By doing so, He became a model of how we are to act when we're mistreated. First Peter 2:21 and 22 says, "For even hereunto were ye called: because Christ also suffered for us, leaving us *an example*, that ye should follow his steps: who did no sin, neither was guile found in his mouth."

The word "example" in verse 21 is from the Greek word *hupogrammos*, which describes *a student who carefully watches his teacher and painstakingly copies what he has done as closely as possible*. Another key word in this passage is the word "steps," which is the Greek word *ichnos*, and it literally means *footprints*. Taken together, these words depict *one putting his or her foot in the exact footprints of someone else*.

This means that in those moments when you feel abused — or have no control over your circumstances and everything is against you — you need to stop, put everything on pause, and think about what Jesus did. He left footprints for you to follow. If you'll place your feet in His steps, studying how He navigated His course and then following His example, you'll do just fine.

STUDY QUESTIONS

> Study to shew thyself approved unto God, a workman that needeth not to be ashamed, rightly dividing the word of truth.
> — 2 Timothy 2:15

1. When other people start playing around with your mind and emotions, are you able to follow Jesus' example by holding your peace and loving them in spite of the torture they're putting you through? God promises to be with and strengthen you. Read what He says in Isaiah 41:10-16. What is He speaking to you through this passage? (Also consider 1 Corinthians 10:13; Philippians 4:6, 7; and James 4:6.)
2. Did you know that Jesus experienced extreme brutality at the hands of the temple police *in addition to* being assaulted later by the religious leaders? How do the details of what He experienced change the way you see Him and what He went through for you?

PRACTICAL APPLICATION

> But be ye doers of the word, and not hearers only, deceiving your own selves.
> — James 1:22

1. Be honest. Are you serious in your relationship with Jesus — or are you, in a sense, like the temple police who played games with Him that night? What evidence confirms your answer?
2. Are you in a situation in which you feel abused or have no control over what's happening in your life? Stop, put everything on pause, and think about what Jesus did. Pray, "Lord, You see this very grueling situation I'm in, and I need Your supernatural strength and wisdom to get through it. If You were me, what would You do?" Be still and listen. What is the Holy Spirit saying?

LESSON 15

TOPIC

Surrender and Release Yourself Into the Loving Care of God

SCRIPTURES

1. **Luke 23:2-4** — ...We found this fellow perverting the nation, and forbidding to give tribute to Caesar, saying that he himself is Christ a King. ...Art thou the King of the Jews? And he answered him and said, Thou sayest it. Then said Pilate to the chief priests and to the people, I find no fault in this man.
2. **Matthew 27:2** — And when they had bound him, they led him away, and delivered him to Pontius Pilate the governor.
3. **Matthew 27:11-14** — And Jesus stood before the governor: and the governor asked him, saying, Art thou the King of the Jews? And Jesus said unto him, Thou sayest. And when he was accused of the chief priests and elders, he answered nothing. Then said Pilate unto him, Hearest thou not how many things they witness against thee? And he answered him to never a word; insomuch that the governor marvelled greatly.
4. **John 18:36** — ...My kingdom is not of this world: if my kingdom were of this world, then would my servants fight, that I should not be delivered to the Jews: but now is my kingdom not from hence.
5. **John 19:12** — And from thenceforth Pilate sought to release him....
6. **Hebrews 9:12** — Neither by the blood of goats and calves, but by his own blood he entered in once into the holy place, having obtained eternal redemption for us.

GREEK WORDS

1. "bound" — (*deo*): to bind, tie up, restrict, imprison; to put in chains; it is the same word that would be used to describe the binding, tying up, or securing of an animal

2. "led him away" — ϖ (*apago*): pictures a shepherd who ties a rope about the neck of his sheep and then leads it down the path to where it needs to go
3. "delivered" — ϖ μ (*paradidomi*): the idea of entrusting something to someone; to commit, to yield, to commend, to transmit, to deliver, or to hand something over to someone else
4. "marvelled" — μ (*thaumadzo*): to wonder; to be at a loss for words; to be shocked and amazed; to be bewildered

SYNOPSIS

As a way of honoring his friend Mark Antony, Herod the Great built the Tower of Antonia in 35 BC on the northeast corner of the Temple Mount in Jerusalem. Standing about 115 feet in height, it was a magnificent military fortress that functioned as a headquarters for a cohort of Roman soldiers, as well as the temple police. Antonia was also the location of Pontius Pilate's palace, the place Christ was finally brought to stand trial before the Roman governor.

The emphasis of this lesson:

Jesus knew it was the Father's will for Him to be the Lamb of God that would take away the sin of the world. Thus, He did not attempt to defend Himself before Pilate or the religious leaders. Secure in the knowledge of His purpose, He entrusted Himself fully to God's loving care.

The Unstable Political and Religious Climate

At the time of Jesus' ministry on earth, Israel was overwhelmed with numerous leaders who were obsessed with power, strategizing ruthlessly day and night on how to remain in control. This grab for power in leadership was true of both the political and religious world. The high priest along with the scribes and elders were paranoid and quickly became suspicious of anyone who appeared to be growing in popularity among the people. The name of the game was control at all costs.

The political leaders over each region were just as paranoid and power-hungry. They were constantly looking over their shoulders and in every nook and cranny for any trace of opposition that would try to steal the reins of power from their hands.

Israel was an occupied territory under Roman rule. The Jews despised the Romans for several reasons. First, the Romans were pagans, and the Jews hated their pagan customs. Second, the Romans had forced them to speak their language, which was not Israel's native tongue. Third, the Romans forced the Jews to pay taxes.

The land of Israel was a hotbed of political turmoil. It was filled with revolts, assassinations, and endless political upheavals. Consequently, few political leaders remained in power for very long. There was always someone lurking behind the scenes, strategizing as to how to subvert and unseat those in authority. The only way a political leader would stay in power for a long time was through the use of cruelty and brutality. It seems that ruthlessness was required for longevity.

Enter Pontius Pilate

The region of Judea made up a large portion of the land of Israel, and it was an extremely unstable environment ruled by a Roman-appointed procurator or governor. Most governors served there for one to three years and then were replaced. This was not the case for Pontius Pilate. He had ruled Judea for *ten* years. This fact alone signifies just how cruel and ruthless he was, and his savagery was confirmed by noted historian Flavius Josephus.

For the entire span of Jesus' three-year ministry, Pilate was governor of Judea. He was the supreme authority in all legal matters throughout the entire territory. Of all the issues brought to him, he most dreaded dealing with cases concerning religion. In fact, he usually referred those cases to the Jewish Sanhedrin because it was their specified jurisdiction.

Pilate lived in Herod's palace in Caesarea. He hated the city of Jerusalem and recoiled at the thought of having to visit there. Its highly religious environment was extremely different from what he was accustomed to, so he stayed in Caesarea as much as possible.

Nevertheless, during the special Jewish feasts, Pilate make his way to Jerusalem with an entourage of military police. The purpose of his visit was not to enjoy the festivities, but to maintain peace and ensure there were no revolts. From Rome's vantage point, that was his number one responsibility. This explains why Pilate was in Jerusalem at the time of Jesus' crucifixion. He was already scheduled to be in the city during the feast of Passover to make sure everything ran smoothly.

Ultimately, there were so many complaints against Pilate filed to the Roman emperor that he was released from his duties and exiled to Gaul, which is modern-day France. Historians say that in the end, he committed suicide. This brutal man who lived a tragic life played a very pivotal role in the life of Jesus and the role of history.

Led Away and Delivered to Pilate

After enduring two intense rounds of brutal abuse at the hands of the temple police and then the religious leaders, "…all the chief priests and elders of the people took counsel against Jesus to put him to death: and when they had bound him, they led him away, and delivered him to Pontius Pilate the governor" (Matthew 27:1, 2).

The word "bound" in verse 2 is the Greek word *deo*, which means *to bind, tie up, restrict, imprison, or to put in chains*. It is the same word that would be used to describe *the binding, tying up, or securing of an animal*. They literally bound Jesus like an animal and led Him to Pilate.

The phrase "led him away" in verse 2 is the Greek word *apago*, which was used to picture *a shepherd who ties a rope about the neck of his sheep and then leads it down the path to where it needs to go*. This is the way the soldiers and temple police led Jesus from Gethsemane to Caiaphas, and it's the same way Caiaphas and the religious leaders led Jesus to Pilate — with a rope wrapped around His neck.

Matthew 27:2 says they "delivered him to Pontius Pilate the governor." The word "delivered" is the Greek term *paradidomi*, which means *to commit, yield, commend, transmit, deliver, or hand something over to someone else*. It carries the idea of *entrusting something to someone*. When Caiaphas sent Jesus to Pilate, he was literally making Jesus Pilate's problem.

The Jews Forced Pilate's Hand

Make no mistake. Caiaphas and his religious cohorts knew exactly what they were doing. They knew Pilate was a cruel, ruthless governor who ruled with an iron fist. They were trying to force his hand to put Jesus to death.

The Jewish people loathed Pilate. For years he had ruled Judea with severe cruelty and brutality, and they'd had their fill. Once they delivered Jesus into Pilate's hands, he would be left with the responsibility of the decision to let Jesus go free or to crucify Him.

By sending Jesus to Pilate, they hoped to not only get rid of Jesus, but also Pilate. They knew if he wouldn't crucify Christ, the charges of treason against him would reach Rome, and he would be removed from his position. Either way, they were going to get something they wanted.

Jesus Refused To Defend Himself

Matthew 27:11 says, "And Jesus stood before the governor: and the governor asked him, saying, Art thou the King of the Jews? And Jesus said unto him, Thou sayest." Jesus' answer was not direct. In fact, it was as if He said, "That's what you say." Instead of defending Himself, He said nothing. This was the *first* chance He passed up to defend Himself.

Then in verse 12, we read, "And when he was accused of the chief priests and elders, he answered nothing." Here, a *second* opportunity came for Jesus to plead His case, but once more He passed on it.

Finally, we come to Matthew 27:13 and 14, which says, "Then said Pilate unto him, Hearest thou not how many things they witness against thee? And he answered him to never a word; insomuch that the governor marvelled greatly." *Three times*, Jesus had opportunity to deny the charges and state His case, and *three times*, He chose not to answer. At this, "…The governor marvelled greatly."

The word "marvelled" is the Greek word *thaumadzo*. It means *to wonder; to be at a loss of words; to be shocked and amazed;* or *to be bewildered*. Pilate was stunned and speechless. He had never seen anyone respond as Jesus did and couldn't understand why He didn't defend Himself. By Roman law, when charges were brought against a person, the person had the legal right to answer the charges and defend himself. If he refused to answer three times, *he was automatically charged as guilty!*

At the end of Pilate's interrogation, he asked Jesus outright, "…Art thou the King of the Jews…?" Jesus answered, saying. "…Thou sayest it" (Luke 23:3). In others words, Jesus told him, "You've said I'm a King, and that's what I am."

This same exchange between Jesus and Pilate is recorded in John's gospel. In fact, in John 18:36, we see that Jesus also said, "…My kingdom is not of this world: if my kingdom were of this world, then would my servants fight, that I should not be delivered to the Jews: but now is my kingdom not from hence."

Pilate just stood there listening, shocked and amazed by what he heard. He was again at a loss for words. "Then said Pilate to the chief priests and to the people, I find no fault in this man" (Luke 23:4).

Pilate's Precarious Position

Clearly, Pilate's political future was in jeopardy. He desperately wanted to remain in control and keep his place of power in Judea, but the situation with Jesus complicated things. The Jews charged Jesus with perverting the nation, claiming to be King, and telling people to withhold their taxes. If Pilate didn't take action against Him, it would be seen as treason and would land him in trouble with Rome.

However, for some reason, he didn't want to take action against Jesus. This ruthless man who had no problem shedding blood in the past seemed to recoil at the idea of charging Jesus with a crime. Was it something in Jesus' behavior? Had Pilate seen something in Jesus' eyes that put a reverential fear of God in him? We don't know for sure.

Nevertheless, Pilate told the chief priests, "…I find no fault in this man" (Luke 23:4). The words "no fault" mean *no cause*. There was *no cause* for taking action against Jesus. This helps us see why the apostle John added, "And from thenceforth Pilate sought to release him…" (John 19:12). Pilate's only chance to avoid making a judgment was to find a legal loophole to set Jesus free.

STUDY QUESTIONS

Study to shew thyself approved unto God, a workman that needeth not to be ashamed, rightly dividing the word of truth.
— 2 Timothy 2:15

1. How does the extreme instability of the political and religious climate during Jesus' day compare with today? How do you think living in that kind of atmosphere as a leader would affect your own relationship with God?

2. What new insights have you gained about Pontius Pilate? How is your perspective of his role in Jesus' crucifixion different after having studied this lesson?

PRACTICAL APPLICATION

> But be ye doers of the word, and not hearers only, deceiving your own selves.
> —James 1:22

1. Jesus was secure in the knowledge of the Father's will for His life and, therefore, entrusted Himself to God's loving care. Why do you think knowing God's will and purpose is so vital?
2. Do you know the Father's will for *your* life in your present season? If so, what is it? If you don't know, stop and pray: "Father, please reveal Your will and purpose for my life. Give me the supernatural ability to cooperate with You so that Your plan becomes a reality and is not thwarted. In Jesus' name."

LESSON 16

TOPIC

Pilate Looks for a Loophole

SCRIPTURES

1. **Matthew 27:2** — And when they had bound him, they led him away, and delivered him to Pontius Pilate the governor.
2. **Matthew 27:11-14** — And Jesus stood before the governor: and the governor asked him, saying, Art thou the King of the Jews? And Jesus said unto him, Thou sayest. And when he was accused of the chief priests and elders, he answered nothing. Then said Pilate unto him, Hearest thou not how many things they witness against thee? And he answered him to never a word; insomuch that the governor marvelled greatly.
3. **Isaiah 53:7 (*NKJV*)** — ...As a sheep before its shearers is silent, so He opened not His mouth.

4. **Luke 23:4-8** — Then said Pilate to the chief priests and to the people, I find no fault in this man. And they were the more fierce, saying, He stirreth up the people, teaching throughout all Jewry, beginning from Galilee to this place. When Pilate heard of Galilee, he asked whether the man were a Galilean. And as soon as he knew that he belonged unto Herod's jurisdiction, he sent him to Herod, who himself also was at Jerusalem at that time. And when Herod saw Jesus, he was exceeding glad: for he was desirous to see him of a long season, because he had heard many things of him; and he hoped to have seen some miracle done by him.
5. **John 18:36** — Jesus answered, My kingdom is not of this world: if my kingdom were of this world, then would my servants fight, that I should not be delivered to the Jews: but now is my kingdom not from hence.
6. **John 19:12** — And from thenceforth Pilate sought to release him....
7. **Hebrews 4:15, 16** — For we have not an high priest which cannot be touched with the feelings of our infirmities; but was in all points tempted like as we are, yet without sin. Let us therefore come boldly unto the throne of grace, that we may obtain mercy, and find grace to help in time of need.

GREEK WORDS

1. "marvelled" — μ (*thaumadzo*): to wonder; to be at a loss of words; to be shocked and amazed; to be bewildered

SYNOPSIS

The Fortress of Antonia, also known as the Tower of Antonia, was located in the northeast corner of the Temple Mount. It was a huge military complex that housed hundreds of Roman soldiers and the temple police. They were stationed there to subdue any uprisings against Rome. Also in this fortress was Pilate's palace — the place Jesus was brought after being brutally abused by Caiaphas and the religious leaders. Jesus' trial before Pilate placed Pilate in a very precarious position.

The emphasis of this lesson:

Pilate was a ruthless, brutal Roman governor. Yet, after hearing and observing Jesus' response to the charges brought against Him, Pilate

found no fault in Him. In fact, from that point on, Pilate sought to set Jesus free. But he needed a legal loophole to justify his action.

After the temple police had brutally abused Jesus, they delivered Him to Caiaphas and about 100 religious leaders. One by one, the religious leaders took turns spitting in Jesus' face as hard as they could. Then they repeatedly struck Him with their fists and slapped Him across the face. The way these religious leaders treated the Son of God behind closed doors is unthinkable. When they had tired of their cruelty, they wrapped a rope around Jesus' neck and led Him like an animal to Pilate.

Matthew 27:2 says, "And when they had bound him, they led him away and delivered him to Pontius Pilate the governor." The word "delivered" is the Greek word *paradidomi*, which means *to commit, yield, commend, transmit, deliver, or hand something over to someone else*. This was the religious leaders' way of saying, "Pilate, we're making Jesus *your* problem."

Jesus Had Three Opportunities To Defend Himself

Delivering Jesus to Pilate created a serious dilemma for him. He was left with the decision to crucify Jesus or set Him free. Matthew 27:11-14 says, "And Jesus stood before the governor: and the governor asked him, saying, Art thou the King of the Jews? And Jesus said unto him, Thou sayest. And when he was accused of the chief priests and elders, he answered nothing. Then said Pilate unto him, Hearest thou not how many things they witness against thee? And he answered him to never a word; insomuch that the governor marvelled greatly."

In four verses, Jesus was given three chances to speak up and plead His innocence. Yet He chose to remain silent and entrust Himself into the Father's care. Isaiah prophesied this more than 700 years earlier, declaring, "…As a sheep before its shearers is silent, so He opened not His mouth" (Isaiah 53:7 *NKJV*).

Pilate "marvelled greatly" at Jesus' silence. The word "marvelled" is the Greek word *thaumadzo*, and it describes *one who is shocked, amazed, baffled, at a loss of words, or completely bewildered*. Pilate had never seen anyone respond in silence as Jesus had. Therefore, he was completely shocked and speechless.

Roman law stated that every accused person had three opportunities to defend himself. If the accused did not speak up and plead his innocence, that person would automatically be convicted as *guilty*. Pilate knew the law, and so did Jesus. The Savior allowed His three opportunities to come and go.

But Pilate was not content to let things simply go in that direction. The Roman governor continued to interrogate Jesus. Luke 23:3 says, "And Pilate asked him, saying, Art thou the King of the Jews? And he answered him and said, Thou sayest it."

In other words, Jesus told Pilate, "You say I am a King, and you are correct." This statement would normally have gotten Jesus in trouble. But after He said this, John's gospel tells us that Jesus went on to say, "…My kingdom is not of this world: if my kingdom were of this world, then would my servants fight, that I should not be delivered to the Jews: but now is my kingdom not from hence" (John 18:36).

What was Pilate's response to Jesus' answers? Luke 23:4 says, "Then said Pilate to the chief priests and to the people, I find no fault in this man." The words "no fault" mean *no cause*. In other words, Pilate was unable to find a reason to convict Jesus as guilty of death. In fact, Pilate was so convinced that Jesus was innocent, John 19:12 says, "And from thenceforth Pilate sought to release him…." The word "sought" means *to aggressively seek*. Immediately, Pilate searched for a way to release Jesus and to simultaneously release himself from the dire predicament he was in.

The Strategy of Vipers

The religious leaders desperately wanted to get rid of Jesus, and they were working a plan to make it happen. They also hated Pilate and wanted him out of the picture. He was a viciously cruel governor who had shed much blood during his tenure. If they were able to remove Pilate in the process of disposing of Jesus, all the better. Their plan had three parts:

Part One: They wanted to see Jesus judged by the Roman court, which would ruin His reputation and guarantee His crucifixion. At the same time, it would vindicate them in the eyes of the people. To ensure that this plan would happen, they falsified two serious political charges against Jesus. First, they claimed that Jesus encouraged the people to withhold their taxes, which wasn't true. Second, they said Jesus claimed to be a king.

If these two charges could be proven, Jesus would be executed for treason against Rome.

Part Two: They wanted to see Pilate removed from office on the grounds that he was unfaithful to the Roman emperor. If Pilate refused to crucify Jesus — a man who claimed to be a rival king — this would make Pilate unfaithful to the Roman emperor. This would be all the ammunition the Jewish leaders needed to prove Pilate should be removed from power. News of his disloyalty would quickly reach Rome, and Pilate would be charged with treason. This charge would lead to Pilate's banishment or death. Therefore, if he let Jesus go free, it guaranteed Pilate would ultimately be removed from power.

Part Three: Regardless of Pilate's decision, the high priest and the religious leaders were planning to take Jesus back to the Sanhedrin and condemn Him to death for blasphemy. They had the religious authority to judge Him and sentence Him to death by stoning for claiming to be the Son of God. The trip to Pilate's court was simply designed to turn Jesus' arrest into a political catastrophe for Pilate. Thus, if Pilate refused to crucify Jesus, they still intended to kill Him. However, if they could use Jesus to first get rid of Pilate, all the better. It is no wonder Jesus called them "vipers." They were slithering, conniving deceivers.

The solution for Pilate was simple: crucify Jesus. That would satisfy the religious leaders and at the same time absolve himself of any possible charge of treason against Rome. But Pilate couldn't bring himself to do it. Even though Jesus had been given three opportunities to defend Himself, yet turned them all down, Pilate struggled with condemning Jesus to death.

Did Pilate see something in Jesus' eyes that instilled a reverential fear of God? Was there something about Jesus' peaceful demeanor that gripped Pilate's heart? Did he feel that Jesus had already been tortured enough by the temple police and religious leaders? We don't know. Nevertheless, Pilate found *no fault* in Jesus and began frantically searching for a loophole to release Him.

Pilate Finds a Loophole

Immediately after Pilate told the chief priests that he found no fault in Jesus, they angrily pushed back. Luke 23:5 tells us, "And they were the more fierce, saying, He stirreth up the people, teaching throughout all Jewry, beginning from Galilee to this place."

There it is, Pilate must of thought. *The loophole I've been looking for!*

Luke 23:6 and 7 reveals, "When Pilate heard of Galilee, he asked whether the man were a Galilean. And as soon as he knew that he belonged unto Herod's jurisdiction, he sent him to Herod, who himself also was at Jerusalem at that time."

Herod Antipas was ruler over the region of Galilee. His palace in Jerusalem had been built by Herod the Great, his father, and it was not far away from the governor's palace. Pilate had found the legal loophole he was looking for to escape the situation. *Since Jesus is a Galilean,* he thought, *Herod should be handling this mess, not me.* So He sent Jesus, with His accusers, to King Herod to hear the matter.

Luke 23:8 says, "And when Herod saw Jesus, he was exceeding glad: for he was desirous to see him of a long season, because he had heard many things of him; and he hoped to have seen some miracle done by him."

In the end, Pilate would not escape having to deal with Jesus, as we will see in our next lesson. Herod would return Him to Pilate, forcing Pilate to make the decision that ultimately sealed Jesus' fate and prophetically fulfilled the Father's plan.

STUDY QUESTIONS

> Study to shew thyself approved unto God,
> a workman that needeth not to be ashamed,
> rightly dividing the word of truth.
> — 2 Timothy 2:15

1. Roman law stated that every accused person had three opportunities to defend himself. If the accused didn't plead his innocence, he was *automatically guilty.* How does this fact change the way you view Pilate's treatment of Jesus and Jesus' response to him?
2. The religious leaders had a three-pronged plan to dispose of Jesus and, if possible, get rid of Pilate in the process. What stands out to you in their strategy? Why do you feel it is significant?

PRACTICAL APPLICATION

> But be ye doers of the word, and not hearers only,
> deceiving your own selves.
> —James 1:22

1. Have you ever been on the receiving end of abuse or been bounced around from one authority figure to another because no one knew what to do with you? Jesus knows exactly how you feel. Take time to pour your heart out to Him and briefly write what you're feeling.
2. Hebrews 4:15 and 16 says, "For we have not an high priest which cannot be touched with the feeling of our infirmities; but was in all points tempted like as we are, yet without sin. Let us therefore come boldly unto the throne of grace, that we may obtain mercy, and find grace to help in time of need." Jesus is here with you right now. Invite Him into your life and your situation. Ask Him to empower you with His divine assistance. Write down anything He speaks to you in these sacred moments.

LESSON 17

TOPIC
Herod Meets Jesus

SCRIPTURES

1. **Isaiah 53:7 (*NKJV*)** — ...As a sheep before its shearers is silent, so He opened not His mouth.
2. **Luke 23:8-10** — And when Herod saw Jesus, he was exceeding glad: for he was desirous to see him of a long season, because he had heard many things of him; and he hoped to have seen some miracle done by him. Then he questioned with him in many words; but he answered him nothing. And the chief priests and scribes stood and vehemently accused him.

GREEK WORDS

1. "saw" — (*horao*): to see; to behold; to delightfully view; to look with the intent to examine; pictures a scrutinizing look
2. "exceeding glad" — (*echare lian*): extreme excitement; the euphoric emotions of someone who is ecstatic about something
3. "desirous" — (*thelo*): to will or to wish; the construction used in this phrase intensifies the wish, making it a very strong wish or desire
4. "a long season" — (*eks hikanon chronon*): for many years; for a long time or for many seasons
5. "miracle" — μ (*semeion*): a sign, a mark, or a token that verifies or authenticates an alleged report; in the Gospels primarily to depict miracles and supernatural events
6. "vehemently" — (*eutonos*): at full pitch; at full volume; strenuously or vigorously; this isn't slightly raising one's voice; this is screaming at full volume in an uncontrolled manner

SYNOPSIS

The Tower of David is located in Jerusalem, and it contains a number of large stones that were once a part of the palace built by Herod the Great a few decades before Christ was born. Herod had several sons — three of them survived him to become rulers of various regions of Israel. Herod Antipas was one of his sons, who lived in the palace built by his father and who ruled over Galilee during the time of Jesus' ministry. Antipas was the Herod Jesus would stand before just before His crucifixion.

The emphasis of this lesson:

Herod Antipas had grown up hearing many stories about Jesus and, therefore, was thrilled for the opportunity to finally meet Him face-to-face. Jesus, however, didn't share Herod's excitement. He not only refused to perform a miracle, He also continued to remain silent before Herod and His accusers.

Judea was filled with sedition, insurrections, riots, and revolts. Typically, a Roman governor ruled there for twelve to thirty-six months. If he lasted three years, it was quite an achievement. In fact, not many rulers made it beyond that point. But Pontius Pilate was different. He ruled for ten years in Judea and obtained a place in history as a result. The reason for his longevity was his ruthless and brutal leadership. Consequently, the Jews despised him and were avidly looking for a way to get rid of Pilate.

A Three-Pronged Plan of Conspiracy

When the Jews attempted to get rid of Christ, they also had a strategy to get rid of Pilate. Their three-pronged plan included:

Part One: The religious leaders wanted to see Jesus judged by the Roman court. This would ruin Jesus' reputation and guarantee His crucifixion. At the same time, it would vindicate them in the eyes of the people. To make this happen, they officially brought two charges against Jesus. First, they said that Jesus had told the people not to pay their taxes, which wasn't true. Second, they said that Jesus claimed to be the "King of the Jews." If they could prove these two charges, then by Roman law, Jesus would have to be executed.

Part Two: In the process of their attempts to dispose of Jesus, the religious leaders wanted to see Pilate removed from office on the charge of being unfaithful to the Roman emperor. If Pilate let Jesus go free, the news of his refusal to crucify a man who claimed to be a rival king would quickly reach the Roman emperor. This would be the ammunition the Jewish leaders needed to prove Pilate should be removed from power. It would be such an offense that the emperor would either banish or execute Pilate.

Part Three: It really didn't matter what Pilate did because the Jews intended to kill Jesus anyway. If Pilate would not crucify Him, they had the authority to take Him back to their Jewish Sanhedrin Court and sentence Him to death for claiming to be the Son of God. By their law, this was blasphemy and worthy of stoning. If Pilate let Jesus go free, it was the best-case scenario for them. Ultimately, Pilate would end up in trouble for treason and be removed, and they themselves would do away with Jesus. It's no wonder Jesus called these Jewish leaders "vipers."

Pilate's Unrest Turned to Relief

When Jesus stood before Pilate, Jesus was given three opportunities to speak and declare His innocence. Nevertheless, He remained silent, fulfilling Isaiah's prophecy, "…As a sheep before her shearers is dumb, so he openeth not his mouth" (Isaiah 53:7). Jesus didn't defend Himself, because He knew it was the Father's will for Him to die on the cross for our salvation.

For some reason, after hearing and observing Jesus, Pilate couldn't bring himself to execute Him. Was it something in Jesus' eyes that instilled a reverential, godly fear? Was it His peaceful, humble demeanor? Was it Jesus' appearance after sweating great drops of blood in Gethsemane and enduring two intense rounds of physical abuse by the temple police and religious leaders? The Bible doesn't say. Nonetheless, Pilate found no fault in Jesus and looked for a loophole to let Him go free.

The instant he learned that Jesus was from Galilee, he was relieved. This fact was the loophole he needed, or so he thought, to get him out of the political conundrum in which he found himself. Luke 23:7 says, "As soon as he knew that he belonged unto Herod's jurisdiction, he sent him to Herod, who himself also was at Jerusalem at that time."

The Herod Family

The Herod family was very large. The most well-known member would be Herod the Great who was alive at the time Christ was born. By the time Jesus had reached the end of His ministry, Herod the Great had been gone for many years. However, he had multiple sons. The three that he didn't put to death out of fear of conspiracy began to rule in his place after his passing. There was *Herod Archelaus* who ruled one part of Israel; *Herod Philip* who ruled parts of northern Israel; and *Herod Antipas* who ruled Galilee and Perea, an area west of the Jordan River.

Herod Antipas was the Herod Jesus stood before hours prior to His crucifixion. Herod had jurisdiction over Galilee, so that is where Pilate sent Him. History shows that Antipas was a very wicked ruler. His name itself is interesting, as it has two possible origins. One possible root for the word "Antipas" is from the word *potter*, which is the Greek word for "fathers."

If "Antipas" came from the word *potter*, it would mean *one who is against fathers*. That is, *one who is against rule or authority* or *one who is against his heritage*. This definition depicts *rebellion and disrespect for authority*.

"Antipas" could also be translated as two words — *anti* and *pas*. The word *pas* means *all*, and the word *anti* means *against*. When you compound the two words to the form the word *antipas*, it means *one who is against everything and everyone*.

So it doesn't matter which interpretation of "Antipas" we take — both origins reveal Herod Antipas was a person with whom it was hard to get along. This is confirmed by historian Flavius Josephus. Antipas disrespected others and was against everyone — parental authority, political authority, *any kind of* authority. Essentially, he was a wicked, cruel tyrant.

Herod Was Excited To See Jesus

When Jesus, the King of kings and the Lord of lords stood in front of Herod Antipas, Herod was euphoric. Luke 23:8 says, "And when Herod saw Jesus, he was exceedingly glad...." The word "saw" is the Greek word *horao*, which means *to see, to behold,* or *delightfully view*. It also can be translated as *a scrutinizing look or to look with the intent to examine.*

So we could translate this part of the verse, "When Herod beheld and delightfully viewed Jesus, he took a scrutinizing look at Him with the intent to examine Him."

This paints a very important picture of what Herod Antipas felt the moment Jesus was finally in front of him. He was *delighted*. He didn't just look at Jesus. He really beheld and examined Jesus and took a scrutinizing view of Him.

Herod was "exceedingly glad" to see Him. "Exceedingly glad" is the Greek phrase *echare lian*, and it describes *extreme excitement*. It pictures *the euphoric emotions of someone who is ecstatic about something*. When Herod saw Jesus, you might say he was "jumping up and down" inside with excitement.

His Wish Had Finally Come True

Why was Herod so excited? Luke 23:8 continues, "...for he was desirous to see him of a long season, because he had heard many things of him; and he hoped to have seen some miracle done by him."

The word "desirous" is the Greek word *thelo*, which describes *a wish or desire*. However, the construction used in this phrase intensifies the wish, making *it a very strong wish or desire*. For a very long time, Herod had wished *desirously* for the opportunity to see Jesus face-to-face. This verse said this had been his desire "of a long season." This phrase in Greek means *for many years* or *for many seasons*.

So why would Herod have such a strong desire to see Jesus in person? The answer is in Luke 23:8 — because "he had heard many things of him...."

Remarkable Stories About Jesus

Jesus was a famous name that had been heard in Herod's household for many years. First, Antipas had heard of **Jesus' supernatural birth**. This was talked about by Herod the Great, Antipas' father. He had been king at the time Jesus was born. His birth was miraculously legendary. That is what Herod Antipas had always heard of Jesus.

Second, he had heard about **the kings from the east who had journeyed from afar** at the time of Jesus' birth. Royalty had recognized the kingship of Christ — they invested their time and treasure to travel to worship Him. This is what Herod had always heard about Jesus.

Third, Antipas had heard about how **his father, Herod the Great, attempted to kill Jesus when he was an infant**. Antipas had been told that Herod killed all the babies in Bethlehem under two years of age, and few escaped his wrath — except Jesus. This was a remarkable truth.

Fourth, Antipas had heard about how **Jesus and His parents escaped into Egypt** and stayed there, waiting for the right moment to return to Israel after the death of his father.

Fifth, Antipas had heard about **the miraculous healing and deliverance ministry of Jesus**. His acts were legendary throughout the land of Israel, even while He was alive on earth. Herod had heard all these amazing stories for years. His father and others as well had talked about Jesus extensively. Yet no immediate family member had actually met Jesus in person — until that moment.

Herod's Cheers Turned to Jeers

Luke 23:8 says, "And when Herod saw Jesus, he was exceeding glad: for he was desirous to see him of a long season, because he had heard many things of him; and he hoped to have seen some miracle done by him."

Herod was hoping to see a "miracle" — the Greek word *semeion*. This describes *a sign, a mark, or a token that verifies or authenticates an alleged report*. It is used in the Gospels primarily to depict *miracles and supernatural events*. Herod wanted to see Jesus do something tangible to authenticate what he had heard about Him for all those years.

However, the Bible says Herod, "…questioned with him in many words; but he answered him nothing. And the chief priests and scribes stood and vehemently accused him" (Luke 23:9, 10). When Jesus just stood there and did nothing, the religious leaders began to "vehemently accuse Him."

The word "vehemently" is the Greek word *eutonos*, which means *at full pitch; at full volume; strenuously or vigorously*. In other words, they didn't *slightly* raise their voices. *They were screaming at full volume in an uncontrolled manner!* We might say the priests and scribes were *screaming their heads off* at Jesus.

When Herod's own cheers turned to jeers, it led to another round of violent assaults against the Lord, which we will examine in our next lesson.

STUDY QUESTIONS

> Study to shew thyself approved unto God, a workman that needeth not to be ashamed, rightly dividing the word of truth.
> — 2 Timothy 2:15

1. The name "Herod" pops up in many places throughout the Gospels. What new insights did you gain concerning the Herodian family? What does the meaning of the name "Antipas" tell you about his character?
2. Reread Luke 23:8-10, including the explanation of the verses in the synopsis. What is the Holy Spirit showing you about Herod and about Jesus in this historical scene?

PRACTICAL APPLICATION

> But be ye doers of the word, and not hearers only, deceiving your own selves.
> — James 1:22

1. Like Herod, have you heard things about Jesus from others, but your personal encounter with Him was not what you expected? What wisdom from Herod's experience can you apply in your own life?
2. Have you ever strongly desired God to speak to you, yet He remained *silent*? What does the reaction of Herod and the religious leaders to Jesus' silence tell you about the condition of their hearts? When God seems to be silent in response to your prayers, what does your reaction reveal about your own heart?

LESSON 18

TOPIC

A Human Ruler Mocks the King of Kings and Lord of Lords

SCRIPTURES

1. **Luke 23:8-11** — And when Herod saw Jesus, he was exceeding glad: for he was desirous to see him of a long season, because he had heard many things of him; and he hoped to have seen some miracle done by him. Then he questioned with him in many words; but he answered him nothing. And the chief priests and scribes stood and vehemently accused him. And Herod with his men of war set him at nought, and mocked him, and arrayed him in a gorgeous robe, and sent him again to Pilate.
2. **John 1:11** — He came unto his own, and his own received him not.

GREEK WORDS

1. "saw" (also "seen") — (*horao*): to see; to behold; to delightfully view; pictures a scrutinizing look; to look with the intent to examine
2. "exceeding glad" — (*echare lian*): extreme excitement; the euphoric emotions of someone who is ecstatic about something
3. "desirous" — (*thelo*): to will or to wish; the construction used in this phrase intensifies the wish, making it a very strong wish or desire
4. "a long season" — (*eks hikanon chronon*): for many years; for a long time or for many seasons
5. "hoped" — ϖ (*elpidzo*): a very strong hope or earnest expectation
6. "miracle" — μ (*semeion*): a sign, a mark, or a token that verifies or authenticates an alleged report; used in the gospels primarily to depict miracles and supernatural events
7. "vehemently" — (*eutonos*): at full pitch; at full volume; strenuously or vigorously; this isn't the slight raising of one's voice; this is screaming at full volume in an uncontrolled manner; these religious

leaders weren't just slightly raising their voices — they were what we might call "screaming their heads off."

8. "men of war" — μ (*strateuma*): a small detachment of Roman soldiers; mostly suggests these men were Herod's personal bodyguards, selected from a larger group of soldiers because they were exceptionally trained and prepared to fight and defend if needed

9. "nought" — (*exoutheneo*): to make one out to be nothing; to make light of, to belittle, disdain, disregard, despise, or treat with malice and contempt

10. "mocked" — μϖ (*empaidzo*): to play a game; often used for playing a game with children or for amusing a crowd by impersonating someone in a silly and exaggerated way; might be used to picture a game of charades when someone intends to comically portray someone or even to make fun of, ridicule, or mock someone; to impersonate someone in a silly and exaggerated way

11. "arrayed" — ϖ (*periballo*): to throw or drape about, as to drape a garment around one's shoulders

12. "gorgeous robe" — μϖ (*estheta lampran*): a garment made of sumptuous, brightly colored, resplendent materials

SYNOPSIS

When Pilate sent Jesus to Herod Antipas, He was taken to Herod's palace in the city of Jerusalem. It was a magnificent structure built by Herod the Great decades earlier. Today, the palace is gone, but many of its stones live on in the construction of the Tower of David, which now stands in place of Herod's palace. If those stones could speak, what would they say to us about the blasphemous abuse Jesus endured at the hands of Herod and the religious leaders?

The emphasis of this lesson:

Herod Antipas and his men of war, along with the chief priests and scribes, treated Jesus dreadfully as He stood before them in Herod's palace. When Christ failed to meet their expectations, they vented their frustrations upon Him. Yet instead of crumbling, Jesus continued to cooperate with the Father's plan to secure our redemption.

Herod Was Excited To See Jesus

Luke 23:8 says, "And when Herod saw Jesus, he was exceeding glad: for he was desirous to see him of a long season, because he had heard many things of him; and he hoped to have seen some miracle done by him." There are several key words in this verse, which we discovered in the last lesson.

The word "saw" is the Greek word *horao*, which means *to see, to behold, or to delightfully view*. It describes *a scrutinizing look* or *a look with the intent to examine*. Herod delightfully beheld Jesus with an examining look. He was "exceedingly glad" to see Him. "Exceedingly glad" is the Greek phrase *echare lian*, which describes *extreme excitement* or *the euphoric emotions of someone who is ecstatic about something*.

Why was Herod so excited? Because he was "desirous to see him of a long season…." The word "desirous" is the Greek word *thelo*, which means *to will* or *to wish*. However, the construction used in this phrase intensifies the wish, making it *a very strong wish or desire*. Herod had a very strong wish "of a long season" to meet Jesus face-to-face. The phrase "of a long season" means Herod had wished for this meeting for *many years* or *for many seasons*. Herod had a driving desire to see Jesus because he had heard many stories about His life.

Five Stories Herod Had Heard

- **Jesus' Supernatural Birth.** Herod Antipas had heard about Jesus' birth from his father, Herod the Great, who had been king at the time of Jesus' birth.
- **The Magi From the East.** Herod had heard about the wise men who came to acknowledge Jesus at His birth. The fact that nobility would travel from the East to celebrate the birth of a child was legendary. The entire Herod family had heard this story, including Antipas.
- **Herod the Great's Attempts To Kill Jesus.** Herod had heard about his father's murderous attempt, during which he killed all the babies in Bethlehem. Jesus managed to escape, which was also legendary because very few people escaped the murderous rampages of Herod the Great.
- **Jesus and His Family's Flight Into Egypt.** Herod had also heard that Jesus' family had slipped out of Israel and stayed in Egypt until

the time of Herod's death. In history, you'll find that Herod the Great was so furious about their escape that he sent spies into Egypt to search for the holy family. That is why the journey of Jesus and his family is often called the "Flight into Egypt." The entire time Joseph, Mary, and Jesus were there, they kept moving from place to place within that nation because Herod doggedly pursued Jesus in order to kill Him. The fact that they escaped his father's wrath was quite amazing to Antipas.

- **Jesus' Miracles and Healing Ministry.** Jesus was a living legend in His own lifetime. Everyone knew about His miraculous works — especially Herod Antipas. Antipas' jurisdiction was Galilee, which was where most of Jesus' miracles took place.

Thus, every member of the Herod family had *heard* of Jesus — but no Herod had ever *met* Jesus except Herod Antipas. Although Herod the Great sought painstakingly to "meet" Jesus in order to kill Him, Antipas was the first to actually look into the face of Jesus. That's why when Jesus stood in front of him, he was "exceeding glad."

In light of all Herod had heard, "…he hoped to have seen some miracle done by him" (Luke 23:8). The word "hoped" — the Greek word *elpidzo* — describes *a very strong hope or earnest expectation.* Herod had an intense expectation that he was going to see Jesus perform a miracle. The word "miracle" is the Greek word *semeion*, which describes *a sign, a mark, or some kind of token that verifies or authenticates an alleged report.* Herod had heard many accounts, but he wanted to personally see something miraculous to authenticate all the alleged reports he'd heard.

Unmet Expectation Became Vocalized Frustration

Luke 23:9 tells us that Herod "…questioned with him in many words; but he answered him nothing." Jesus refused to perform on demand. Instead, He remained silent. To this, "…the chief priests and scribes stood and vehemently accused him" (v. 10).

The word "vehemently" is the Greek word *eutonos*, which means *at full pitch*; *at full volume*; *strenuously*; or *vigorously*. This doesn't describe people *slightly* raising their voices; this pictures people *screaming at full volume in an uncontrolled manner.* These religious leaders weren't just slightly raising their voices — they were what we might call "screaming their heads off."

The Bible says the chief priests and scribes "accused" Him. "Accused" is from the Greek word *kategoreo*, which means *to accuse with evidence; to bring legal charges against*; or *to accuse before a judge*. The religious leaders turned Herod's palace into a courtroom, judging Jesus and saying things like, "He's no miracle worker; He's just a charlatan." Screaming uncontrollably, they verbally assaulted Him with their venomous words. Yet that was not the end of it.

Herod and His Henchmen Joined In

Luke 23:11 states, "And Herod with his men of war set him at nought, and mocked him, and arrayed him in a gorgeous robe, and sent him again to Pilate." Along with the religious leaders, Herod and his "men of war" joined in the attack.

The phrase "men of war" is the Greek word *strateuma*, which describes *a small detachment of Roman soldiers*. Most scholars agree these men were Herod's personal bodyguards, selected from a larger group of soldiers because they were exceptionally well-trained to fight and defend if necessary. Hence, Herod, the dignified and well-educated ruler of Galilee, and his bodyguards, who were well armed and also highly educated, began to behave like maniacs.

They "set Him at nought." The word "nought" is from the Greek word *exoutheneo*, which means *to make one out to be nothing; to make light of; to belittle, disdain, disregard, despise, or treat with malice and contempt*. It carries the idea of *totally demolishing something*. In other words, these leaders were literally trying to demolish Jesus with their verbal attacks. These intelligent, sophisticated men were violently screaming at Jesus, tearing Him to shreds with their words.

They also "mocked" Him. "Mocked" is the Greek word *empaidzo*, which means *to play a game* — it's the same word used to describe what the temple police did to Jesus. *Empaidzo* was often used for *playing a game with children* or for *amusing a crowd by impersonating someone in a silly and exaggerated way*. This word might be used in a game of charades when someone intends to comically portray someone or even to make fun of, ridicule, or mock someone.

When Jesus refused to perform a miracle, Herod and his men of war likely began pretending to be Jesus healing people. They also probably impersonated someone being healed. They were playing games at Jesus' expense, mocking Him to destroy Him and make Him out to be nothing in their presence.

Herod and the religious leaders "arrayed Him in a gorgeous robe." The word "arrayed" is the Greek word *periballo* — a compounding of the word *peri*, meaning *around*, and the word *ballo*, meaning *to cast or throw*. Together these two words form the word *periballo*, which means *to throw or to drape about, as to drape a garment around one's shoulders*.

What kind of garment did they throw around Jesus? Verse 11 says a "gorgeous robe" — the Greek phrase *estheta lampran*, which describes *a garment made of sumptuous, brightly colored, resplendent materials*. This was very often used to describe *the clothing of a king or a politician*. Being in Herod's palace gave them access to such clothing. To complete their game of charades with Jesus, Herod and his men of war draped a "gorgeous robe" around His shoulders and sent Him back to Pilate.

By doing so, Herod was saying, "Jesus is no king. He's just another pretender running for office." Christ endured this horrible treatment even though He had done nothing wrong. For three years He had given His life, serving His people. John 1:11 says, "He came unto his own, and his own received him not." The very people who mocked and abused Jesus brutally were among the very people He died for on the cross.

STUDY QUESTIONS

> Study to shew thyself approved unto God, a workman that needeth not to be ashamed, rightly dividing the word of truth.
> — 2 Timothy 2:15

1. The stories Herod had heard about Jesus regarding His supernatural ability to heal and work wonders were all true. Yet when Jesus stood before Herod, He didn't perform any miraculous signs. Did Jesus' inactivity change His ability to do the impossible? What does this say to you about His timing and purpose for performing miracles in *your* life? (Consider Psalm 31:14-17; Ecclesiastes 3:1, 11; Acts 1:7, 8; and Galatians 4:4.)

2. Jesus stood before Herod, his men of war, and the religious leaders, enduring their verbal abuse without saying a word. He wasn't afraid of them, nor was He affected by their words. He knew something deep in His heart that we need to know in our own hearts. Read John 13:3;

Second Timothy 1:12; Hebrews 7:25; and Jude 1:24 to discover this treasured revelation.

PRACTICAL APPLICATION

> But be ye doers of the word, and not hearers only, deceiving your own selves.
> —James 1:22

1. Herod Antipas and the religious leaders violently took out their frustrations on Jesus when He failed to meet their expectations. Be honest. How do you tend to react when Jesus fails to meet *your* expectations? How does seeing their reaction help you see your own feelings and reactions in a different light?
2. Like Jesus, has there been a time in your life when people verbally or physically abused you because you didn't meet their demands? If so, briefly describe the situation. How have you responded?

LESSON 19

TOPIC

Charged, But Not Guilty

SCRIPTURES

1. **Luke 23:11** — And Herod with his men of war set him at nought, and mocked him, and arrayed him in a gorgeous robe, and sent him again to Pilate.
2. **Luke 23:14-16** — …Ye have brought this man unto me, as one that perverteth the people: and, behold, I, having examined him before you, have found no fault in this man touching those things whereof ye accuse him: No, nor yet Herod: for I sent you to him; and, lo, nothing worthy of death is done unto him. I will therefore chastise him, and release him.
3. **Luke 23:18-23** — …Away with this man, and release unto us Barabbas: (who for a certain sedition made in the city, and for murder, was cast into prison.) Pilate therefore, willing to release Jesus, spake again to them. But they cried, saying, Crucify him, crucify him. …Why,

what evil hath he done? I have found no cause of death in him: I will therefore chastise him, and let him go, but they were instant with loud voices, requiring that he might be crucified. And the voices of them and of the chief priests prevailed.

4. **John 19:12** — …If thou let this man go, thou art not Caesar's friend: whosoever maketh himself a king speaketh against Caesar.
5. **Matthew 27:24** — When Pilate saw that he could prevail nothing, but that rather a tumult was made, he took water, and washed his hands before the multitude, saying, I am innocent of the blood of this just person: see ye to it.

GREEK WORDS

1. "set him at nought" — (*exoutheneo*): to make one out to be nothing; to make light of, to belittle, to disdain, to disregard, to despise, or to treat with malice and contempt
2. "mocked" — μω (*empaidzo*): to play a game; often used in the context of playing a game with children or amusing a crowd by impersonating someone in a silly and exaggerated way; might be used to depict a game of charades when someone comically portrays someone else or even makes fun of, ridicules, or mocks another person; to impersonate someone in a silly and exaggerated way
3. "arrayed" — ω (*periballo*): to throw or to drape about, as to drape a garment around one's shoulders
4. "gorgeous robe" — μω (*estheta lampran*): a garment made of sumptuous, brightly colored, resplendent materials
5. "examined" — (*anakrino*): to examine closely; to scrutinize; to judge judicially
6. "sedition" — (*stasis*): treason; a deliberate attempt to overthrow the government or to kill a head of state
7. "murder" — (*phonon*): premediated murder; intentional killing; a calculated slaughter; a planned massacre
8. "cast" — (*ballo*): to throw; to hurl
9. "prison" — (*phulake*): prison or place of confinement or containment; a Roman prison was one of the most dreaded places in the Roman empire
10. "cried" — ω (*epiphoneo*): to shout, scream, yell, shriek, or screech; the Greek tense means they were hysterically screaming

and shrieking at the top of their voices — totally out of control and without pause

11. "saying" — (*legontes*): the tense used means they were endlessly pleading, demanding, and imploring
12. "they were instant" — ω μ (*epikeimai*): to pile on top of
13. "tumult" — (*thorubos*): an uproar; trouble that throws things into disorder; emotions that are out of control; a public outcry that is accompanied by shrieks and hysterical wailing; a disturbance that results in panic and a breach of public order; a public disturbance
14. "was made" — μ (*ginomai*): something that comes to pass unexpectedly; an event that is unanticipated and therefore surprising
15. "innocent" — (*athoos*): guiltless; free of blame or guilt; unpunishable
16. "before" — ω (*apenanti*): publicly; in the sight of

SYNOPSIS

The Tower of Antonia, or the Antonia Fortress, was located less than a mile from Herod's palace in Jerusalem. Positioned on the northeast corner of the Temple Mount, it housed the palace of Pontius Pilate. After Pilate had sent Jesus to Herod, Herod sent Jesus back to Pilate. Although both leaders found Jesus innocent, ultimately He would be charged and sentenced to death by Pilate. The will of the people would prevail, despite Jesus being guiltless.

The emphasis of this lesson:

After Herod and his bodyguards finished their verbal assassination of Jesus, Herod sent Him back to Pilate. Standing by his original verdict, Pilate again declared Jesus innocent. But when the mob grew violently out of control and he saw his job was on the line, Pilate gave the people what they screamed for — the release of Barabbas and the death of Jesus.

When Jesus refused to perform a miracle for Herod, Luke 23:11 says, "Herod with his men of war set him at nought...." The "men of war" were Herod's well-trained bodyguards. The phrase "set him at nought" is from the Greek word *exoutheneo*, meaning *to make one out to be nothing; to belittle, to disdain, to disregard, to despise,* or *to treat with malice and contempt.*

These sophisticated, educated people lost all sense of decency and began to act like animals, trying to verbally demolish Jesus with their words.

Then they "mocked" Him. "Mocked" is from the Greek word *empaidzo*, which means *to play a game. It was often used for playing a game with children or for amusing a crowd by impersonating someone in a silly and exaggerated way.* This word might be used to depict a game of charades when someone comically portrays someone else or even makes fun of, ridicules, or mocks another person.

After they set Jesus at *nought* and *mocked* Him, Luke 23:11 says, they "arrayed him in a gorgeous robe, and sent him again to Pilate." The word "arrayed" is the Greek term *periballo*, meaning *to throw to drape about, as to drape a garment around one's shoulders.* The phrase "gorgeous robe" is from the Greek phrase *estheta lampran*, which describes *a garment made of sumptuous, brightly colored, resplendent materials.* Putting the robe around Jesus was Herod's way of saying, "Jesus is no king. He's just another pretender — another *'wannabe'* running for office."

Jesus — Back in Pilate's Court

Although Herod was deeply disappointed that Jesus wouldn't perform a miracle for him, he could find no legal charges to bring against Him. After Herod and his bodyguards were done with their mockery and blasphemous behavior toward Jesus, Herod sent Him back to Pilate. Again, the "Jesus" decision Pilate was hoping to avoid landed in his lap.

When Jesus' returned to the Tower of Antonia, Pilate reassembled the religious leaders in the court. He then addressed them saying, "…Ye have brought this man unto me, as one that perverteth the people: and, behold, I, having examined him before you, have found no fault in this man touching those things whereof ye accuse him: No, nor yet Herod: for I sent you to him; and, lo, nothing worthy of death is done unto him. I will therefore chastise him, and release him" (Luke 23:14-16).

Pilate said he "examined" Jesus. "Examined" is from the Greek word *anakrino*, which means *to examine closely, to scrutinize, or to judge judicially.* Pilate examined Jesus and found no "fault" in Him. That is, he found *no cause for action* against Jesus.

Pilate was the highest legal authority in the land — no one was higher. He knew Roman law, and it was his duty to ensure it was fully obeyed. From a judicial standpoint, he couldn't find a single crime Jesus had committed worthy of death. To bolster his findings, Pilate added that Herod *also* couldn't find any fault in Jesus.

In an attempt to satisfy the people, Pilate ordered Jesus to be scourged. Basically, he said, "If you want to see blood, I'll give you blood. I'll have Jesus scourged. But I don't want to kill Him. I'll chastise Him and let Him go." However, this wasn't enough. The religious leaders demanded Christ's death.

It was the custom at that time of Passover for one prisoner to be released as a favor to the people. All of Jerusalem would wait with anticipation to see who would be released. With this in mind, the religious leaders and the people cried out in unison against Jesus, "…Away with this man, and release unto us Barabbas" (Luke 23:18).

Who Was Barabbas?

Luke 23:19 says Barabbas, "who for a certain sedition made in the city, and for murder, was cast into prison." The word "sedition" is from the Greek word *stasis*, which means *treason*. It is *a deliberate attempt to overthrow the government or to kill a head of state*. Barabbas had tried to kill someone who was the head of the local government — possibly Pontius Pilate himself. For this reason, the locals probably saw Barabbas as a hero, as they hated the Romans. Even so, Barabbas was extremely dangerous.

Barabbas was also thrown in prison for "murder," which is the Greek word *phonon*. This word indicates *premediated murder, an intentional killing, a calculated slaughter, or a planned massacre*. Thus, Barabbas was a bona fide terrorist! He had been proven guilty of premeditated murder, attempting to assassinate a head of state, and avidly working to overthrow the government.

As a violent criminal, Barabbas had been "cast into prison." The word "cast" is from the Greek word *ballo*, meaning *to throw* or *to hurl*. The word "prison" is the Greek word *phulake*, which describes *a Roman prison — a place of confinement or containment*. This was one of the most dreaded places in the Roman Empire. Barabbas was so dangerous that as soon as the authorities put their hands on him, they hurled him into a Roman prison.

Ironically, the thing Barabbas had been tried and convicted of — treason and trying to overthrow the government — by the religious leaders. Yet they screamed, "Give us Barabbas and crucify Jesus!" In effect, they said, "Release to us the man who *really* committed treason, and execute the Man in whom you find no fault"!

Pilate Pleads Jesus' Cause

Luke 23:20 and 21 says, "Pilate therefore, willing to release Jesus, spake again to them. But they cried, saying, Crucify him, crucify him." Pilate earnestly longed to release Jesus, but the people "cried" to have Him crucified. The word "cried" is the Greek word *epiphoneo*, which is a compound of the words *epi*, meaning *upon*, and *phoneo*, meaning *a loud voice*. When compounded to form *epiphoneo*, it means *to shout, to scream, to yell, to shriek*, or *to screech*. The Greek tense here means they were hysterically screaming and shrieking at the top of their voices — totally out of control and without pause.

In verse 21, Luke also uses the word "saying." He said the people "cried, saying, Crucify him, crucify him." This word is from the Greek word *legontes*. The tense used here means they were *endlessly pleading, demanding, and imploring* to have Jesus executed.

Pilate said to the crowd the third time, "…Why, what evil hath he done? I have found no cause of death in him: I will therefore chastise him, and let him go, and *they were instant* with loud voices, requiring that he might be crucified. And the voices of them and of the chief priests prevailed" (Luke 23:22, 23).

The Bible says "they were instant" with their voices, from the Greek word *epikeimai*, which is a compound of the word *epi*, meaning *upon*, and *keimai*, meaning *to pile*. When these two words are joined to become *epikeimai*, it means *to pile on top of*. The screaming voices of the people began "to pile on top of" Pilate — the roar of their demands nearly *suffocating* and *burying* him.

John 19:12 adds that the people also said, "…If thou let this man go, thou art not Caesar's friend: whosoever maketh himself a king speaketh against Caesar." Remember, one of the charges they brought against Jesus was that He claimed to be the king of the Jews. Pilate knew if he let Jesus go free, he would be viewed as a traitor by Rome, and Pilate would either be banished or executed for not being faithful to the emperor.

Pilate Absolved Himself of All Guilt

Matthew 27:24 says, "When Pilate saw that he could prevail nothing, but that rather a tumult was made, he took water, and washed his hands before the multitude, saying, I am innocent of the blood of this just person: see ye to it."

The more Pilate tried to plead Jesus' case and let Him go, the more riotous the crowd became. Matthew 27:24 says "a tumult was made." The word "tumult" is the Greek word *thorubos*, which describes *an uproar; trouble that throws things into disorder; emotions that are out of control; a public outcry that is accompanied by shrieks and hysterical wailing; or a disturbance that results in panic and a breach of public order*. This scene had turned into a public disturbance of mega proportions that neither Rome nor Pilate would permit.

The words "was made" in verse 24 are from the Greek word *ginomai*, which describes *something that comes to pass unexpectedly; an event that is unanticipated and therefore surprising*. The situation with Jesus rapidly mushroomed in to an uproar Pilate never anticipated. As soon as he saw the explosiveness of the situation, he decided to give the people what they wanted — but not before washing his hands.

The Bible says Pilate washed his hands "before the multitude." The word "before" is the Greek word *apenanti*, which means *publicly in the sight of everyone*. When Pilate washed his hands, he said, "I am innocent." The word "innocent" is the Greek word *athoos*, which means *guiltless; free of blame or guilt; unpunishable*. Pilate said, "I'm not guilty of this Man's death. I'm innocent and absolved of guilt." He then turned Jesus over to the religious leaders — giving them exactly what they wanted. Jesus was then scourged and crucified. He died on Golgotha for the sin of humanity, including your sin and mine.

STUDY QUESTIONS

Study to shew thyself approved unto God, a workman that needeth not to be ashamed, rightly dividing the word of truth.
— 2 Timothy 2:15

1. Living to please people can be very dangerous. God warns us about this in Deuteronomy 1:17; Proverbs 29:25; Isaiah 51:12, 13; and Luke 12:4, 5. What is the Holy Spirit showing you in these passages?

2. Barabbas was a known criminal, guilty of treason and murder. Yet he was set free and Jesus, the innocent One, was sentenced to death. In what ways can you identify with Barabbas — one who was guilty and worthy of death, but who was set free because Jesus took his place?

PRACTICAL APPLICATION

> But be ye doers of the word, and not hearers only, deceiving your own selves.
> —James 1:22

1. In an attempt to satisfy the people, and for fear of what would happen to him, Pilate gave in to the crowd's demands. He went against what he knew in his heart was right — that Jesus was innocent. Is there an area in your life where you are doing this? If so, where?
2. For what reasons have you compromised what you know to be right? Pause and pray, "Holy Spirit, what is the root cause for my actions? Of what am I afraid? What can I do to cooperate with You and see a change in my life?"

LESSON 20

TOPIC

The Horror of a Roman Scourging

SCRIPTURES

1. **Matthew 27:24** — When Pilate saw that he could prevail nothing, but that rather a tumult was made, he took water, and washed his hands before the multitude, saying, I am innocent of the blood of this just person: see ye to it.
2. **Isaiah 52:14** — As many were astonied at thee; his visage was so marred more than any man, and his form more than the sons of men.
3. **Matthew 27:26-31** — Then released he Barabbas unto them: and when he had scourged Jesus, he delivered him to be crucified. Then the soldiers of the governor took Jesus into the common hall, and gathered unto him the whole band of soldiers. And they stripped him, and put on him a scarlet robe. And when they had platted a crown of

thorns, they put it upon his head, and a reed in his right hand: and they bowed the knee before him, and mocked him, saying, Hail, King of the Jews! And they spit upon him, and took the reed, and smote him on the head. And after that they had mocked him, they took the robe off from him, and put his own raiment on him, and led him away to crucify him.

4. **Isaiah 53:5** — But he was wounded for our transgressions, he was bruised for our iniquities: the chastisement of our peace was upon him; and with his stripes we are healed.
5. **First Peter 2:24** — ...By whose stripes ye were healed.

GREEK WORDS

1. "tumult" — (*thorubos*): an uproar, tumult; trouble that throws things into disorder; emotions that are out of control; a public outcry that is accompanied by shrieks and hysterical wailing; a disturbance that results in panic and a breach of public order; a public disturbance
2. "was made" — μ (*ginomai*): something that comes to pass unexpectedly; an event that is unanticipated and therefore surprising
3. "innocent" — (*athoos*): guiltless; free of blame or guilt; unpunishable
4. "before" — ϖ (*apenanti*): publicly; in the sight of
5. "scourged" — (*phragelloo*): one of the most horrific words used in the ancient world because of the terrible images that immediately came to mind when a person heard this word; to flog; to scourge
6. "band of soldiers" — ϖ (*speira*): a military cohort composed of a tenth part of a legion; well-trained Roman soldiers who were equipped with the finest weaponry of the day
7. "scarlet" — (*kokkinos*): the most expensive garment in the ancient world; pictures a garment dyed in purple; the color or kind of a garment worn by high-ranking officials, politicians, generals, or emperors
8. "stripes" — μ (*molops*): a full-body bruise; a terrible lashing that draws blood and that produces discoloration and swelling of the entire body

9. "healed" — μ (*iaomai*): a word that refers to physical healing; borrowed from the medical world to describe the physical healing or curing of the human body

SYNOPSIS

Located in the city of Jerusalem is the Church of the Holy Sepulchre. Encased behind thick glass in this church, a section of a column is featured. Some historians believe it to be a section of the column to which Jesus was tied when He was scourged by Roman soldiers. A close look at this granite column reveals laceration marks left by a scourging. Whips made of multiple leather straps with pieces of metal, bone, and glass at each end cut grooves into that stone column. Just imagine what happened to the fleshly body of Jesus when He was thusly beaten?

The emphasis of this lesson:

Jesus didn't just receive a few lashes across His back. His entire body was literally torn open by the Roman scourge. The grueling abuse He received from Gethsemane to Calvary is beyond what any human being could endure. Yet He bore it all for you and me and all humanity.

What Does It Mean to Be Scourged?

In his book, *Paid in Full: An In-Depth Look at the Defining Moments of Christ's Passion*, Rick writes:

> The word "scourged" is the Greek word *phragelloo*. It was one of the most horrific words used in the ancient world because of the terrible images that immediately came to mind when a person heard it….
>
> When a decision was made to scourge an individual, first the victim was first stripped *completely* naked so his entire flesh would be open and uncovered to the beating action of the torturer's whip. Then the victim was bound to a two-foot high scourging post. His hands were tied over his head to a metal ring, and his wrists were securely shackled to that ring to restrain his body from movement. When in this locked position, the victim couldn't wiggle or move, trying to dodge the lashes that were laid across his back.

Romans were professionals at scourging. They took special delight in the fact that they were the "best" at punishing a victim with this brutal act. Once the victim was harnessed to the post and stretched over it, the Roman soldier began to put them through unimaginable torture. One writer notes that the mere anticipation of the whip caused the victim's body to grow rigid, the muscles to knot in his stomach, the color to drain from his cheeks, and his lips to draw tight against his teeth as he waited for the first sadistic blow of the whip that would begin tearing his body open.

The scourge itself consisted of a short wooden handle with several 18- to 24-inch-long pieces of leather protruding from it. The ends of these pieces of leather were equipped with sharp pieces of metal, glass, wire, and jagged fragments of bone. This was considered to be one of the most feared and deadly weapons of the entire Roman world. It was so ghastly that the mere threat of scourging could calm a crowd or bend the will of the strongest rebel. Even the most hardened criminals recoiled from the prospect of being submitted to the vicious beating of a Roman scourge.

Most often, two torturers were utilized to carry out the punishment, simultaneously lashing the victim from both sides. As these dual whips struck the victim, the leather straps with their sharp jagged objects descended and extended over his entire back. Each piece of metal, wire, bone, or glass cut deeply through the victim's skin and into his flesh, shredding his muscles and sinews.

Every time the whip pounded across the victim, those straps of leather curled torturously around his torso, biting painfully and deeply into the skin of his abdomen and upper chest. As each stroke lacerated the sufferer, he tried to thrash about but was unable to move because his wrists were held so firmly to the metal ring above his head. Helpless to escape the whip, he would scream for mercy that the anguish might come to an end.

Every time the torturers struck the victim, the straps of leather attached to the wooden handle would cause multiple lashes as the sharp objects at the end of each string sank deep into the flesh and then raked across the victim's body. Then the torturer would jerk back, pulling hard enough to tear out whole pieces of human flesh from the body. The victim's back, buttocks, back of the legs, stomach, upper chest, and face would soon be disfigured by the slashing blows of the whip.

Historical records describe a victim's back as being so mutilated after a Roman scourging that his spine would actually be exposed. Others recorded how the bowels of a victim would spill out through the opened wounds created by the whip. The Early Church historian Eusebius wrote, "The veins were laid bare, and the very muscles, sinews, and bowels of the victim were open to exposure."

…With so many blood vessels sliced open by the whip, the victim would begin to experience a profuse loss of blood and bodily fluids. The heart would pump harder and harder, struggling to get blood to the parts of the body that were bleeding profusely. But it was like pumping water through an open water hydrant; there was nothing to stop the blood from pouring through the victim's open wounds.

This loss of blood caused the victim's blood pressure to drop drastically. Because of the massive loss of bodily fluids, he would experience excruciating thirst, often fainting from the pain or going into shock. Frequently, the victim's heartbeat would become so irregular that he would go into cardiac arrest.

This was a Roman scourging.

According to Jewish law in Deuteronomy 25:3, the Jews were permitted to give 40 lashes to a victim, but because the fortieth last usually proved fatal, the number of lashes given was reduced to 39…. But the Romans had no limit to the number of lashes they could give a victim, and the scourging Jesus experienced was at the hands of Romans, not Jews. Therefore, it is entirely possible that after the torturer pulled out his whip to beat Jesus, he may have laid more than 40 lashes across His body. In fact, this is even probably in light of the explosive outrage the Jews felt for Jesus and the terrible mocking He had already suffered at the hands of Roman soldiers.

So when the Bible tells us that Jesus was scourged, we know exactly what type of beating Jesus received that night. What toll did the cruel Roman whip exact on Jesus' body? The New Testament doesn't tell us exactly what Jesus looked like after He was scourged, but Isaiah 52:14 says, "As many were astonished at thee; his visage was so marred more than any man, and his form more than the sons of men." If we take this scripture literally for what it says, we can conclude that Jesus' physical body was marred nearly beyond recognition.... This scourging was only the preparation for Jesus' crucifixion![1]

It Was a Grueling Night for Jesus

The agony Jesus went through was so much more than just the cross. It began when He was in Gethsemane. He knew what lay ahead, and in great agony of the soul, He sweat great drops of blood. After being betrayed by Judas and turned over to the religious leaders, Jesus was taken by the temple police who beat, slapped, and mocked Him. He was then led to Caiaphas' palace, where the religious leaders repeatedly spit on Him, beat Him with their fists, and slapped Him across the face.

The temple police then led Jesus to Pontius Pilate, who interrogated Him and found Him without fault. Not knowing what to do with Jesus, he sent Him to Herod once he heard Jesus was a Galilean.

Again, Jesus was mocked and verbally assassinated — this time by Herod, his bodyguards, and the religious leaders. After they were done with their charades, Herod sent Jesus back to Pilate.

Pilate knew Jesus was innocent and earnestly longed to set Him free, but when the noise of the crowd became a riotous tumult, Pilate gave the people what they wanted. After washing his hands, symbolically declaring himself guiltless, He gave the orders for Jesus to be scourged and then crucified on Golgotha.

Robed To Be Ridiculed

Matthew 27:26 and 27 says, "...And when he had scourged Jesus, he delivered him to be crucified. Then the soldiers of the governor took Jesus into the common hall, and gathered unto him the whole band of soldiers."

The phrase "band of soldiers" is from the Greek word *speira*, which describes *a Roman cohort of soldiers*. That was *a tenth part of a legion*, or *about 600 well-trained soldiers who were equipped with the finest weaponry of the day*. This band of soldiers came together to mock Jesus. Matthew 27:28 says, "And they stripped him, and put on him a scarlet robe."

There Jesus was — His body shredded from the Roman scourging. His muscles, tendons, and veins exposed — His blood flowing out of His body from multiple lacerations. And in the midst of His severe suffering, nearly 600 soldiers stripped Him naked and put a scarlet robe on Him.

The word "scarlet" is the Greek word *kokkinos*. It describes *the most expensive garment in the ancient world — a garment dyed in purple*. This was *the color or kind of a garment worn by high-ranking officials, politicians, generals, or emperors*. The word "robe" in the Greek refers to *a cloak worn by soldiers, military officers, magistrates, kings, or emperors*. The soldiers would have secured this garment from Pilate's wardrobe, which they had access to while in his palace. Their actions were nothing more than utter mockery.

Crowned With Deadly Thorns

Then in Matthew 27:29, it says, "And when they had platted a crown of thorns, they put it upon his head, and a reed in his right hand: and they bowed the knee before him, and mocked him saying, Hail, King of the Jews!"

The word "thorns" describes a plant of thorns so sharp that by itself could cause delirium or possibly even death when one was pierced by it. The soldiers took these thorns and "put it upon his head." The phrase "put upon" is the Greek word *epitithimi*, which means *to forcibly thrust or to shove*. In other words, the soldiers shoved a woven crown of long, sharp thorns onto the head of Jesus, causing intense pain and profuse bleeding.

With a scarlet robe around His shoulders, a crown of thorns on His head, and a reed placed in His right hand, the soldiers recreated a mockery of a famous statue of the Roman Emperor Caesar. Then the Scripture says that, one by one, they "bowed the knee before him, and mocked him…."

It didn't end there. Matthew 27:30 tells us, "They spit upon him, and took the reed, and smote him on the head." As before, the soldiers got right up in Jesus' face and spit as hard as they could. Then they "smote" Him on the head with the reed. "Smote" in the Greek means *to beat, to strike*, or *to violently smack*. "And after that they had mocked him, they took the robe off from him, and put his own raiment on him, and led him away to crucify him" (Matthew 27:31). Again, the word "led" is the Greek word *apago*, which is the word used to describe *a shepherd who ties a rope around the neck of his sheep and leads it down the path it is supposed to go.*

He Endured It All for Our Healing

Peter recalled from memory the scourging Christ received. He declared in First Peter 2:24, "…By whose stripes ye were healed." The word "stripes" is the Greek word *molops*, and it describes *a full-body bruise; a terrible lashing that draws blood and that produces discoloration and swelling of the entire body.* Peter was there and saw this take place with his own eyes.

The prophet Isaiah foretold of Jesus' scourging more than 700 years before it took place, saying, "But he was wounded for our transgressions, he was bruised for our iniquities: the chastisement of our peace was upon him; and *with his stripes we are healed*" (Isaiah 53:5).

The word "healed" in First Peter 2:24 is the Greek word *iaomai*, which always refers to *physical healing*. It is borrowed from the medical world to describe *the physical healing or curing of the human body.* Jesus endured the horrific Roman scourge that produced a full-body bruise so that you and I and every believer would be physically healed — utterly redeemed from sickness and disease. Because of Jesus' scourging, we can experience the redemptive blessing of healing in Christ.

STUDY QUESTIONS

> **Study to shew thyself approved unto God, a workman that needeth not to be ashamed, rightly dividing the word of truth.**
> **— 2 Timothy 2:15**

1. Prior to this lesson, what was your understanding of the whipping Jesus received? Of all the new insights you have learned, what touched you most deeply? Why?
2. How has this fresh perspective of the Roman scourging that Jesus endured impacted your love and appreciation for Him?
3. When you think about God's promise of healing, what scriptures come to mind? (Consider Psalm 103:3; Proverbs 4:20-22; James 5:14-16.)

PRACTICAL APPLICATION

> But be ye doers of the word, and not hearers only, deceiving your own selves.
> —James 1:22

1. First Peter 2:24 declares that by Jesus' stripes, you were healed. He paid an unbelievably high price to purchase our physical healing. Have you been tolerating sickness somewhere in your body? If so, where? Are you ready to stand on God's promise of healing, proclaiming His truth until it becomes a reality in your life?
2. In the eyes of society, to wash one's hands as Pilate did absolved them of guilt and made them unpunishable for their actions. Do you think God sees this the same way? Why or why not? Explain your answer.

[1] Rick Renner, *Paid in Full: An In-Depth Look at the Defining Moments of Christ's Passion*, 2008. 3rd printing 2015 (Harrison House), 170-173.

LESSON 21

TOPIC
Crucified

SCRIPTURES

1. **Matthew 27:26** — ...and when he had scourged Jesus, he delivered him to be crucified.
2. **Philippians 2:8** — And being found in fashion as a man, he humbled himself, and became obedient unto death, even the death of the cross.
3. **Matthew 27:35, 36** — ...parted his garments, casting lots.... And sitting down they watched him there.
4. **John 19:23, 24** — Then the soldiers, when they had crucified Jesus, took his garments, and made four parts, to every soldier a part; and also his coat: now the coat was without seam, woven from the top throughout. They said therefore among themselves, Let us not rend it, but cast lots for it, whose it shall be....

5. **1 Peter 1:18, 19** — Forasmuch as ye know that ye were not redeemed with corruptible things, as silver and gold, from your vain conversation received by tradition from your fathers; but with the precious blood of Christ, as of a lamb without blemish and without spot.

GREEK WORDS

1. "scourged" — (*phragelloo*): one of the most horrific words used in the ancient world because of the terrible images that immediately came to mind when a person heard this word; to flog; to scourge
2. "crucified" — (*stauros*): pictures an upright, pointed stake that was used for the punishment of criminals; used to describe those who were hung up, impaled, or beheaded and then publicly displayed; always used in connection with public execution
3. "watched" — (*tereo*): to guard; the Greek tense means to consistently guard or to consistently be on watch

SYNOPSIS

Jesus Christ was crucified more than 2,000 years ago on the hill called Golgotha. For centuries that followed, churches were built atop Golgotha, memorializing the place where Jesus gave His life for our redemption. The story is true and the location is real. Historical evidence proves that Jesus really lived and really died a dreadful death — a death by crucifixion.

The emphasis of this lesson:

Crucifixion was a ghastly, torturous death reserved for criminals. Jesus died this kind of death for us. He was nailed to the cross and bore the sin of humanity in Himself. He gave His life's blood to redeem us. We must always remember what He went through for us.

Before Jesus made His way to Golgotha, Pilate had Him scourged. As we learned, the word "scourged" is the Greek word *phragelloo*, and it was one of the most horrific words used in the ancient world because of the terrible images that immediately came to mind when a person heard this word. Jesus' body was literally ripped open and shredded — *scourged* — by the whips of the Roman soldiers. They lacerated His body, causing blood to pour out from every cut and gaping wound.

First Peter 2:24 says that by His "stripes" we were healed. The word "stripes" is the Greek word *molops*. It describes *a full-body bruise; a terrible lashing that draws blood and that produces discoloration and swelling of the entire body*. That is what Jesus went through for all humanity. Matthew 27:26 says, "...And when he had scourged Jesus, he delivered him to be crucified."

The Act of Crucifixion

The word "crucified" was taken from the Greek word *stauros*, which describes *an upright, pointed stake that was used for the punishment of criminals*. Historically, only criminals were crucified. This confirms Isaiah 53:12, which stated that Jesus would die a criminal's death. The word "crucified" was also used to describe those who were *hung up, impaled, or beheaded and then publicly displayed*. It was always used in connection with public execution, and the purpose of the execution was to humiliate the person being crucified.

Crucifixion was one of the cruelest and most barbaric forms of punishment in the ancient world. Flavius Josephus described crucifixion as the most wretched of all deaths. At the time that Jesus was crucified, the act of crucifixion was entirely in the hands of Roman authorities. This punishment was reserved for the most serious offenders, usually for those who had committed some act of treason or who had participated in or sponsored state terrorism.

The following paragraphs present three additional facts about this wretched act of crucifixion.

1. The Crossbeam and the Nails

Once the offender reached the place where the crucifixion was to occur, he was laid on the crossbeam that he carried himself. Soldiers would then stretch the victim's arms out and drive a five-inch iron nail through each of his wrists. It was not through the palm of his hands, but through his wrists and into the crossbeam.

After being nailed to the crossbeam, the victim and the beam were hoisted by a rope, and the crossbeam was dropped into a notch on the top of the upright post. When the crossbeam dropped into the groove, the victim suffered excruciating pain as his hands and wrists were wrenched by the sudden jerking motion. Eventually, the weight of the victim's body caused his arms to be pulled from their sockets.

Once the victim's wrists were secured in place on the crossbeam — and the beam was hoisted and notched atop the post — the feet came next. The victim's legs would be positioned so that the feet were pointed downward with the soles pressed against the post on which he was suspended. A long nail would then be driven between the bones of the feet. The nail was lodged firmly enough between those bones to prevent it from tearing through the feet as the victim arched upward gasping for breath.

2. The Process of Asphyxiation

In order for the victim to breathe, he had to push himself up by the feet, which were nailed to the vertical post. Because the pressure in his feet became unbearable, it was impossible to remain in that position for very long. Eventually, he would collapse back into the hanging position.

As the victim pushed up and collapsed back down again and again over a long period of time, his shoulders eventually dislocated and popped out of joint. Soon afterward, the elbows and wrists would follow. The various dislocations caused the arms to be extended up to nine inches longer than normal, often resulting in terrible cramps in the victim's arm muscles and making it impossible for him to push himself up any longer to breathe. When he was finally too exhausted and could no longer push himself up using the nail lodged in his feet, the process of asphyxiation began.

Jesus experienced all of this torture. When He dropped down with the full weight of His body on the nails that were driven through His wrists, it sent horrific pain up His arms that registered in His brain. Added to this torture was the agony caused by the constant grating of His back that had just been scourged. Every time He pushed Himself up to breathe and then collapsed back into a hanging position, His back grated against the upright post.

Due to the extreme loss of blood and hyperventilation, a victim would begin to experience severe dehydration. We can see this in Jesus' own crucifixion when He cried out in John 19:28 and said, "I thirst." After several hours of this torment, the victim's heart would begin to fail. Next his lungs would collapse and the excess fluid would begin filling the lining of his heart and lungs, adding to the slow process of asphyxiation. A person who was crucified eventually drowned as his own fluids filled his lungs.

3. The Purpose in Breaking the Victim's Legs

When the Roman soldier came to determine whether or not Jesus was alive or dead, he thrust his spear into Jesus' side. One expert noted that if Jesus had been alive when the soldier did this, the soldier would have heard a loud sucking sound caused by air being inhaled past the freshly made wound in the chest. But the Bible tells us that water and blood mixed together came pouring forth from the wound the spear had made in Jesus' side, which was evidence that Jesus' heart and lungs had shut down and were now filled with fluid. It was enough to assure the soldier that Jesus was already dead.

It was customary for Roman soldiers to break the lower leg bones of a person being crucified to make it impossible for the victim to push himself upward to breathe and thus causing him to asphyxiate at a much quicker rate. However, because of the blood and the water that gushed from Jesus' side, He was already considered dead. So there was no reason for the soldier to hasten Jesus' death by breaking His legs. Thus, His legs were never broken.

This is a brief taste of Roman crucifixion. It is exactly what Jesus experienced on the cross. In Philippians 2:8, Paul said, "And being found in fashion as a man, he humbled himself, and became obedient unto death, even the death of the cross." The emphasis in this verse is on the word "even." In Greek, the word "even" is the word *de*, which dramatizes the point that *Jesus lowered Himself to such an extent that He died even the death of the cross.*

Soldiers Cast Lots and Watched Jesus

Matthew 27:35 says, "And they crucified him, and parted his garments, casting lots: that it might be fulfilled which was spoken by the prophet, They parted my garments among them, and upon my vesture did they cast lots."

Roman law required that the person being crucified was to be stripped naked. Thus, when Jesus was crucified, He hung naked on the cross. This was part of the humiliation. And according to Roman custom, the soldiers who carried out the crucifixion had a right to the victim's clothes.

The gospel of John says, "Then the soldiers, when they had crucified Jesus, took his garments, and made four parts, to every soldier a part; and also his coat: now the coat was without seam, woven from the top throughout. They said therefore among themselves, Let us not rend it, but cast lots for it…" (John 19:23, 24).

After the soldiers finished casting lots, Matthew 27:36 says, "And sitting down they watched him there." The word "watched" is the Greek word *tereo*, which means *to guard*. The Greek tense here means *to consistently guard* or *to consistently be on the watch*. It was the responsibility of these soldiers to maintain order at the crucifixion site. Specifically, they were on duty to ensure no one came to rescue Jesus from the cross.

As Jesus hung there, nails through His wrists and feet, gasping for His next breath, the soldiers at the foot of the cross were oblivious to what was happening. They simply didn't understand the great price of redemption that was being paid by Jesus.

Always Remember What Jesus Went Through for You

In reality, the cross of Jesus Christ was a disgusting, revolting, nauseating sight. It was a horrific, humiliating punishment reserved for the most hardened criminals. No one in the ancient world wanted anything to do with it.

Today, our society has taken the cross and turned it in to a fashion item. It adorns ears, hangs on chains, and is even tattooed on people's skin. It has been decorated with diamonds, encrusted with jewels, and forged in gold and other precious metal. To a great degree, by beautifying the cross, we have forgotten the true picture of what Christ endured as He hung there and died a slow, torturous death.

His flesh had been ripped to shreds — his wounds had become a full-body bruise from head to toe. His hair, His face, His beard, and His body all oozed blood from the multiple lacerations and gaping wounds left behind by the scourging. A crown of delirium-inducing thorns had been shoved onto His head. Nails had been driven through His wrists and feet. And for every breath He breathed, He had to push up the full weight of His body by exerting pressure on the nail through His feet. The pain Jesus suffered was indescribable.

That was just the physical agony. Jesus also bore the emotional and mental pain of carrying the sin of the entire human race. Second Corinthians 5:21 tells us that Jesus, who knew no sin, *became* sin so that we might become the righteousness of God in Christ. The weight of the sin of the world was heavier than the scourging and the cross. But He did it all for us.

As believers, it is good for us to take time to reflect on what Jesus Christ's death on the cross was really like. When we fail to remember what it cost Him to save us and heal us, we begin to lose our gratitude for Him and can even treat our salvation carelessly. It is only when we deliberately choose to remember all Jesus went through that we can begin to sincerely appreciate the almost inconceivable price He paid for our redemption.

The apostle Peter wrote to remind us of this, saying, "Forasmuch as ye know that ye were not redeemed with corruptible things, as silver and gold, from your vain conversation received by tradition from your fathers; but with the precious blood of Christ, as of a lamb without blemish and without spot" (1 Peter 1:18, 19).

Remember, Easter is not about bunnies, eggs, and candy. It is about the death, burial, and resurrection of Jesus — the event that is at the very core of our faith. So understand the cross, embrace the cross, and thank God for the cross of Jesus Christ!

STUDY QUESTIONS

Study to shew thyself approved unto God, a workman that needeth not to be ashamed, rightly dividing the word of truth.
— 2 Timothy 2:15

1. What did you learn from this lesson about the crucifixion that you didn't previously know?
2. As Jesus experienced the Roman scourging, the crown of thorns, the nails in His wrists and feet, and the spear in His side, a tremendous amount of blood was shed. Take a moment to think about it. What does the blood of Jesus mean to *you* personally? (Consider Romans 5:9; Colossians 1:19-22; Hebrews 9:11-14; 10:19-22; 1 John 1:7.)

PRACTICAL APPLICATION

But be ye doers of the word, and not hearers only, deceiving your own selves.
— James 1:22

1. Many people today have turned the symbol of the cross, the instrument of Jesus' death, into a fashion item. What are your thoughts regarding this?
2. From your perspective, what would you say are the personal benefits of taking time to remember the scourging, the abuse, and the crucifixion Jesus endured at the hands of the religious leaders and the Roman soldiers?
3. There are people all around you who don't know Jesus and are heading for an eternity in hell. Jesus died and paid the price so they could avoid that. How does this lesson motivate and encourage you to share the Good News of Jesus with others?

LESSON 22

TOPIC
It Is Finished

SCRIPTURES
1. **Matthew 27:26** — ...and when he had scourged Jesus, he delivered him to be crucified.
2. **Philippians 2:8** — And being found in fashion as a man, he humbled himself, and became obedient unto death, even the death of the cross.
3. **John 19:30** — When Jesus therefore had received the vinegar, he said, It is finished: and he bowed his head, and gave up the ghost.
4. **Hebrews 9:12** — Neither by the blood of goats and calves, but by his own blood he entered in once into the holy place, having obtained eternal redemption for us.
5. **Isaiah 53:4, 5** — Surely he hath borne our griefs, and carried our sorrows: yet we did esteem him stricken, smitten of God, and afflicted. But he was wounded for our transgressions, he was bruised for our iniquities: the chastisement of our peace was upon him; and with his stripes we are healed.

GREEK WORDS
1. "scourged" — (*phragelloo*): one of the most horrific words used in the ancient world because of the terrible images that immediately came to mind when a person heard this word; to flog; to scourge
2. "crucified" — (*stauros*): pictures an upright, pointed stake that was used for the punishment of criminals; used to describe those who were hung up, impaled, or beheaded and then publicly displayed; always used in connection with public execution
3. "It is finished" — (*Tetelestai*): to bring to completion; to bring to a conclusion; to complete; to accomplish; to fulfill or to finish; marks a turning point when one period ended and another period began

SYNOPSIS

The Church of the Holy Sepulchre is located in the city of Jerusalem adjacent to Golgotha, the hill upon which Jesus was crucified. The word "Golgotha" means *the place of the skull*. The reason this hill is called Golgotha is quite interesting. According to Jewish history and some early Christian writers, this was the place where *Adam* was buried. Origen, an early Christian scholar and theologian, wrote in the early Second Century that Jesus was crucified above Adam's burial site. If this is true, this is significant, especially in light of the events described in Matthew 27:51-54.

The moment Jesus died, there was a great earthquake. Evidence of the quake can be seen in the bedrock of Golgotha today. As noted, some early Christian writers stated that when Christ died atop Golgotha, His blood seeped down through the fissures caused by the quake and made its way to the skull of Adam. According to their view, this symbolically represents Jesus' blood being shed to cover the sins of the entire human race. Jesus, the Last Adam, covered everything done by the first Adam.

The emphasis of this lesson:

Jesus' final words "It is finished!" were very telling. When He shouted this phrase, He was conveying four significant messages at that defining moment of His sacrifice: *His mission was accomplished*; *atonement was completed*; *our debt was paid in full*; **and** *a new beginning had come*.

Before being crucified on Golgotha, Jesus was brutally scourged at Pilate's command (*see* Matthew 27:26). As we've seen previously, the word "scourged" is from the Greek word *phragelloo*, meaning *to flog* or simply *to scourge*. This was one of the most horrific words used in the ancient world because of the terrible images conjured in a person's mind when he heard it. This cruel, vicious punishment of scourging was inflicted by the hands of Roman soldiers. The Romans took great pride in the fact that they were the best at scourging a victim. When Jesus was scourged, His body was literally shred and ripped open by the soldiers' whips.

After the scourging, Jesus was taken to be "crucified." This word is derived from the Greek word *stauros*, which actually describes *an upright, pointed stake that was used for the punishment of criminals*. The fact that Jesus was crucified and publicly displayed indicates He was seen and treated as a criminal. The word "crucified" was also used to describe *those who were hung up, impaled, or beheaded and then publicly displayed*. Crucifixion was always used in connection with public execution.

In Philippians 2:8, the apostle Paul talked about Jesus, saying, "And being found in fashion as a man, he humbled himself, and became obedient unto death, *even* the death of the cross." In Greek, the word "even" is the word *de*, and it is a very important word. In fact, this verse could be better translated: "He humbled Himself and became obedient unto death. *If you can possibly imagine it,* He went to such great lengths that He even died the miserable, despised death of a cross."

Marred Beyond Recognition

Approximately 700 years before Christ was crucified, the prophet Isaiah foretold of Jesus' physical appearance on the cross. In Isaiah 52:14, he said, "As many were astonied at thee; his visage was so marred more than any man, and his form more than the sons of men." And in Isaiah 53:2, Isaiah prophesied that Jesus "...hath no form nor comeliness; and when we shall see him, there is no beauty that we should desire him."

Jesus had been put through an immeasurable amount of torture from the moment of His arrest in Gethsemane to the time of His last breath on the cross. He had been abused and battered, torn and tattered by one hateful group after another. In the end, the Bible says His appearance was marred more than any other. His entire body was disfigured and mangled to such a degree He no longer looked human.

Continuing His prophecy about Jesus, Isaiah said, "He is despised and rejected of men; a man of sorrows, and acquainted with grief: and we hid as it were our faces from him; he was despised, and we esteemed him not" (Isaiah 53:3). All that Christ endured made it unbearable to look at Him. His appearance was so ghastly that people turned and hid their faces from Him.

Why would Jesus endure such shocking cruelty? Why would He allow Himself to be beaten and abused beyond human recognition? The answer is, *He did it for us.* "Surely he hath borne *our* griefs, and carried *our* sorrows: yet we did esteem him stricken, smitten of God, and afflicted. But he was wounded for *our* transgressions, he was bruised for *our* iniquities: the chastisement of *our* peace was upon him; and with his stripes we are healed" (Isaiah 53:4, 5).

All Christ did, He did for *our* benefit.

Jesus Cried, 'It Is Finished!'

The very last words Jesus uttered from the cross are captured in John 19:30. It says, "When Jesus therefore had received the vinegar, he said, It is finished: and he bowed his head, and gave up the ghost." The phrase "it is finished" is a translation of the Greek word *tetelestai*, which means *to bring to completion; to bring to a conclusion; to complete; to accomplish; to fulfill or finish*. It is a form of the Greek word *telos*, which describes *anything that has arrived at completion, maturity, or perfection.*

There are many nuances to the word *tetelestai*, but here are four primary meanings conveyed in Jesus' last words that have significance for this defining moment of His supreme sacrifice.

Meaning One: Mission Accomplished

In biblical days, when a servant was sent on a mission, upon his return, he would report to his master, "Tetelestai." The very word that Jesus exclaimed on the cross — translated "it is finished" — was the same word a servant would say to his master.

Once the servant finished the assignment, he would say to his master, "Tetelestai," meaning, "I've done exactly what you requested" or, "The mission is now accomplished." When Jesus cried out and said, "Tetelestai

— it is finished," He was exclaiming to the entire universe that He had faithfully fulfilled the Father's will. The mission was accomplished.

No wonder Jesus shouted those words. This was the greatest victory in the history of the human race. He had been faithful to His assignment even in the face of overwhelming challenges. Now the fight was over, and Jesus could cry out to the Father, "Tetelestai — it is finished!" His mission was accomplished.

Meaning Two: Atonement Is Completed

The second meaning of the word *tetelestai* ("it is finished") is related to the temple sacrifices. Every year the high priest presented a sacrificial lamb without spot or blemish to atone for the sins of Israel. He would then enter the Holy of Holies where he poured the blood of the sacrificial, spotless lamb on the mercy seat of the Ark of the Covenant. The instant that blood touched the mercy seat, atonement was made for the people's sins for another year. In that moment, the high priest would say, "Tetelestai," meaning, *"The sacrifice is complete. Atonement for the sins of Israel is accomplished."*

When Jesus hung on the cross, He was both the *Lamb* and *High Priest*. In that moment, our Great High Priest offered up His own blood for the permanent removal of sin. He offered up the perfect sacrifice, of which every preceding sacrifice was a type and a symbol. From then on, there was no more need for any additional sacrifices for sin. Jesus was the final sacrifice.

He then entered into the Holy Place in Heaven and offered up His own blood — a sacrifice so complete that God never again required the blood of lambs for granting forgiveness. Thus, when Jesus cried out, 'Tetelestai — it is finished," He was declaring the end of all sacrifices. The ultimate Sacrifice had finally been made. Atonement was completed, perfected, and fully accomplished. It was done once and for all — finished forever.

Meaning Three: Paid in Full

The third meaning of *tetelestai*, "it is finished," is connected to the secular business world. Here, it was a word used to signify *the full payment of a debt*. When a debt had been fully paid off, the parchment on which the debt was recorded was stamped with the word *Tetelestai*, indicating "it is finished." This meant the debt had been paid in full.

In a spiritual sense, this means that once a person calls Jesus the Lord of his life and personally accepts His sacrifice, no debt of sin exists for that person any longer. Jesus paid the price for sin that no sinner could ever pay. Through His death on the cross, the debt was wiped away: *Tetelestai* — "it is finished!"

Jesus took our place and paid the sin-debt we owed. He paid with the currency of His own blood, and when we, by faith, repent and receive Him as Lord, we are set free. He stamps our sin-debt "Paid in Full" because of the sacrifice He made on the cross.

So when Jesus uttered those words, "It is finished," it was the equivalent of His declaring that the sin-debt was fully satisfied, fulfilled, and complete. His blood utterly and completely cleansed us forever. It was far-reaching and all-embracive for all of us who put our faith in Him.

Meaning Four: A New Beginning

The fourth meaning of *tetelestai*, "it is finished," depicted *a turning point when one period ended and new period began.*

When Jesus exclaimed, "It is finished!" it was a turning point in the entire history of mankind. At that exact moment, He was declaring that the time of the Old Testament had come to an end — it was finished and closed — and the time of the New Testament had begun. The cross "marks the spot" of this great divide in human history.

The moment Jesus shouted, "Tetelestai" or, "It is finished!" the Old Testament prophecies about His life and ministry were fulfilled. The justice of God had been fully met and satisfied by the Lamb of God. The sacrifices of the Old Testament permanently ceased because the Perfect Sacrifice had laid down His life for the salvation of mankind. Jesus' mission was complete. The old had passed away and the new had come.

Christ Paid the Entire Price — *in Full!*

Isaiah 53:4 and 5 says, "Surely he hath borne our griefs, and carried our sorrows: yet we did esteem him stricken, smitten of God, and afflicted. But he was wounded for our transgressions, he was bruised for our iniquities: the chastisement of our peace was upon him; and with his stripes we are healed."

This means you can know and be confidently assured that:

- if you're consumed with grief, *Jesus bore your grief.*
- if you're overwhelmed with sorrow, *He carried your sorrows.*
- if you're trapped in a life of transgression, *He was wounded for your transgressions.*
- if you're living in sin, you can be forgiven because *He was bruised for your iniquities.*
- if you're tormented and have no peace, *He was chastised for you to have peace.*
- if you're physically or mentally sick, *He was scourged with stripes for your healing.*

Christ paid the price for your freedom and total restoration with His own blood on the cross. Hebrews 9:12 says, "Neither by the blood of goats and calves, but by his own blood he entered in once into the holy place, having obtained eternal redemption for us."

I encourage you to pause and think about the terrific price Jesus paid — and to, by faith, embrace everything He purchased for you in His death and resurrection. He didn't suffer everything He went through so you would be miserable in life. He suffered and died so you might live and experience the freedom for which He paid.

STUDY QUESTIONS

Study to shew thyself approved unto God, a workman that needeth not to be ashamed, rightly dividing the word of truth.
— 2 Timothy 2:15

1. Carefully reread and contemplate Isaiah 53:2-5 along with Philippians 2:5-8. What is the Holy Spirit speaking to you about the character and person of Jesus in these passages?
2. In Romans 5:14-19, the first Adam is contrasted with Christ, who came to undo all the first Adam did through disobedience. Carefully read this passage and identify what entered the human race through Adam's offense and what resulted from Christ's selfless act of obedience. (Also consider Paul's comparison in First Corinthians 15:45-49.)

PRACTICAL APPLICATION

> But be ye doers of the word, and not hearers only, deceiving your own selves.
> —James 1:22

1. Take a moment to write down the four primary meanings of the words "it is finished" (*tetelestai*). Of the four, which one is most meaningful to you? Why?
2. Before going through this lesson, had you ever heard that Jesus' physical appearance was marred and mangled beyond recognition (*see* Isaiah 52:14)? How does this knowledge affect your perception of Him and your devotion to Him?

LESSON 23

TOPIC
Buried and Sealed

SCRIPTURES

1. **John 19:41, 42** — Now in the place where he was crucified there was a garden; and in the garden a new sepulchre, wherein was never man yet laid. There laid they Jesus … the sepulchre was nigh at hand.
2. **Matthew 27:60** — And laid it in his own new tomb, which he had hewn out in the rock: and he rolled a great stone to the door of the sepulchre, and departed.
3. **Isaiah 53:9** — And he made his grave with the wicked, and with the rich in his death; because he had done no violence, neither was any deceit in his mouth.
4. **Luke 23:55** — And the women also, which came with him from Galilee, followed after, and beheld the sepulchre, and how his body was laid.
5. **Mark 15:47** — …beheld where he was laid.
6. **Matthew 27:63-66** — …Sir, we remember that that deceiver said, while he was yet alive, After three days I will rise again. Command therefore that the sepulchre be made sure until the third day, lest his

disciples come by night, and steal him away, and say unto the people, He is risen from the dead: so the last error shall be worse than the first. Pilate said unto them, Ye have a watch: go your way, make it as sure as ye can. So they went, and made the sepulchre sure, sealing the stone, and setting a watch.

7. **Acts 2:23, 24** — ...Ye have taken, and by wicked hands have crucified and slain [Jesus]: whom God hath raised up, having loosed the pains of death: because it was not possible that he should be holden of it.

GREEK WORDS

1. "garden" — ϖ (*kepos*): any garden with trees and spices; an orchard; the same word is used to describe the garden of Gethsemane, which was an olive-tree orchard
2. "nigh" — (*engus*): nearby; close at hand
3. "new" — (*kainos*): fresh or unused
4. "hewn" — μ (*latomeo*): to cut out, but to polish; implies a special, highly developed, refined tomb; pictures a tomb that was splendid and expensive (Matthew 27:60; Mark 15:46; Luke 23:53)
5. "laid" — μ (*tithimi*): to set, to lay, to place, to deposit, or to set in place
6. "beheld" — μ (*theaomai*): to gaze upon; to fully see; to look at intently; it is where we get the word "theater"
7. "how" — (*hos*): careful contemplation; very careful observance
8. "sure" — (*sphragidzo*): pictures a legal seal placed on documents, letters, possessions — or, in this case, a tomb; its purpose was to authenticate that the sealed item had been properly inspected before sealing and that all contents were in order; as long as the seal remained unbroken, it guaranteed that the contents inside were safe, sound, and undisturbed
9. "watch" — (*koustodia*): a guard or watch; pictures a group of four Roman soldiers whose shift changed every three hours
10. "sure" — (*asphalidzo*): to provide added security; to assure that security is achieved

SYNOPSIS

There is quite an interesting history surrounding the tomb of Jesus. When the Emperor Hadrian came to power in 117 AD, he began destroying every remnant of Judaism and Christianity that still existed in Jerusalem. For instance, he so abhorred Judaism that he had a temple built to Zeus in the place where the Jewish temple once stood. And when he discovered the tomb of Jesus, he built a temple to the goddess Aphrodite on top of it to try to hide it forever.

Many years later, when Constantine became emperor, he and his mother, Helena, began restoring all the sacred Christian sites. He gave orders to demolish and remove the temple of Aphrodite, and when they did, they found the tomb of Jesus. Hadrian's attempts to conceal the tomb actually served to preserve it. Constantine would oversee the building of the Church of the Holy Sepulchre on this sacred site.

Christians have been visiting this historic site for nearly 1,700 years. Although there are other locations that claim to be the burial place of Jesus, the Church of the Holy Sepulchre has been historically identified from the earliest years as the place of Christ's burial.

The emphasis of this lesson:

The death of Jesus Christ was not a hoax. He really died on the cross and was buried in the tomb of Joseph of Arimathea. To ensure Jesus was dead and to prevent His disciples from stealing His body, the religious leaders acquired permission from Pilate to seal the tomb and to post Roman soldiers to guard it.

During a time after Christ's resurrection, there were circulating rumors that He never actually died — that He had been alive when He was placed inside that tomb, and simply "came out" after He had rested and recovered. Others alleged that Christ's disciples came and stole His body from the grave and then *claimed* that He had been resurrected.

But Jesus' death was no hoax. Just as He really lived, He also really died. And three days later He was raised back to life! These truths are historical, well-documented, and central to everything we believe.

Jesus Was Buried in a Rich Man's Tomb

John 19:41 says, "Now in the place where he was crucified there was a garden; and in the garden a new sepulchre, wherein was never man yet laid." The word "garden" is the Greek word *kepos*, and it describes *any garden with trees and spices.* It can also mean *an orchard.* It is the same word used to describe the garden of Gethsemane, which was an olive-tree orchard.

So there was a beautiful garden near the place of the crucifixion, and in the garden was a "new sepulchre." The word "new" is the Greek word *kainos*, which describes *something fresh or unused.* There was a fresh, never-before-used tomb in the garden that had recently been chiseled out of the rock.

Matthew 27:57 through 60 tells us the tomb belonged to "…a rich man of Arimathea, named Joseph, who also himself was Jesus' disciple…." Then it says Joseph "…went to Pilate, and begged the body of Jesus. Then Pilate commanded the body to be delivered. And when Joseph had taken the body, he wrapped it in a clean linen cloth, and laid it in his own new tomb, which he had hewn out in the rock…."

Notice the word "hewn." This is the Greek word *latomeo*, which means *to cut out of rock, and to highly polish*. It implies *a special, highly developed, refined tomb* or *a tomb that was splendid and expensive.* Only wealthy individuals could own tombs of this nature. Most people in Israel were buried in simple tombs with hinged doors — not a tomb hewn out of rock. Interestingly, the fact that this tomb was hewn out of rock is mentioned in Matthew 27:60; Mark 15:46; and Luke 23:53. This repeated fact confirms that Joseph of Arimathea was a very wealthy man.

The prophet Isaiah noted this in Isaiah 53:9, saying, "And he made his grave with the wicked, and with the rich in his death; because he had done no violence, neither was any deceit in his mouth."

The Men Laid Him to Rest

Joseph had recently had this tomb hewn for himself, but since he was still alive and Jesus had died, he dedicated the use of his own tomb to Christ. John 19:42 says, "There laid they Jesus therefore because of the Jews' preparation day; for the sepulchre was nigh at hand."

The word "laid" is important. It is the Greek word *tithimi*, which means *to set, to lay, to place, to deposit,* or *to set in place.* It is used in this verse to describe how they very carefully placed Jesus' body in its resting place inside the tomb.

Joseph of Arimathea and his friend Nicodemus had ceremonially cleansed the body of Jesus and then wrapped it with about 100 pounds of spices, preparing Him for burial (*see* John 19:38-40). They spent hours hovering over Him during this process. If there had been even a flicker of a pulse or a whisper of breath left in Jesus' lungs, they would have seen it. But there was none. Christ was dead.

The Women Carefully Observed Him

The men were not alone. Luke 23:55 says, "And the women also, which came with him from Galilee, followed after, and beheld the sepulchre, and how his body was laid." The word "beheld" is the Greek word *theaomai*, and in this verse it means *to gaze upon*, *to fully see*, or *to look at intently*. It is where we get the word *theater*.

By using this word "beheld," it indicates that the women didn't rush in and rush out of the tomb. Instead, they watched every act and movement of his burial — as if they were in a theater. With eyes wide open, they saw "how" Jesus' body was laid. The word "how" is the Greek word *hos*, which describes *careful contemplation and very careful observance*. They intently gazed on the burial of Jesus and observed everything about it.

Mark's gospel verifies this, saying, "And Mary Magdalene and Mary the mother of Joses beheld where he was laid" (Mark 15:47). Here, the word "beheld" is used in a slightly different tense. Specifically, it means *they continually gazed upon Jesus*.

This verse could be translated, *"They carefully contemplated where and how He was laid."* That is, they stayed there awhile and took their time to look upon the body of Jesus in its burial cloths and to reflect. The reason they paused and pondered was that they didn't think they would ever see Him again. This was their final farewell to the One they loved deeply.

After Joseph had carefully laid Jesus' body in the fresh stone tomb and everyone said goodbye, Matthew 27:60 says Joseph "rolled a great stone to the door of the sepulchre, and departed." As far as they were concerned, that was the end of it.

The Religious Leaders Were Afraid

Although sorrow gripped the hearts of the disciples, *fear* gripped the hearts of the religious leaders. They were very concerned that somehow Jesus' death was a hoax or that His disciples would come at night and steal His body and then claim He was resurrected. Matthew 27:62-64 explains:

Now the next day, that followed the day of preparation, the chief priests and Pharisees came together unto Pilate, saying, Sir, we remember that that deceiver said while he was yet alive, After three days I will rise again. Command therefore that the sepulchre be made sure until the third day, lest his disciples come by night, and steal him away, and say unto the people, He is risen from the dead; so the last error shall be worse than the first.

Notice what the religious leaders requested: "Command therefore that the sepulchre be made sure...." The word "sure" is the Greek word *sphragidzo*, and it describes *a legal seal placed on documents, letters, and possessions*. In this passage, the seal was placed upon *a tomb*. The purpose of a "sure" seal was to authenticate that the sealed item — in this case, Jesus' body — had been properly inspected before sealing and that all contents were in order. As long as the seal remained unbroken, it guaranteed that the contents inside were safe, sound, and undisturbed.

More than likely, the religious leaders were asking that a string of some kind be stretched across the entrance of the tomb and sealed on both sides by Pilate's official seal. He was the governor of Judea, and no one was higher in authority than him. Therefore, his seal was very powerful and important. No one dare break the seal that was put in place by Pontius Pilate.

An Inspection Was Required, and Jesus' Death Was Legally Authenticated

According to the word "sure" (*sphragidzo*), the tomb couldn't be sealed until they first checked its contents. For this to happen, the religious leaders, along with Roman soldiers and officials from Pilate's court had to go to the tomb and reopen it. They had to roll away the stone, enter the tomb, and check everything to make sure everything was in order so they could seal it.

Keep in mind that Joseph of Arimathea, Nicodemus, and the women were unaware that this was taking place. As far as they knew, they had carefully prepared Jesus' body for burial, laid Him to rest, and sealed the tomb with the large stone.

But Pilate's officials along with the Roman soldiers and religious leaders went to the tomb, rolled back the stone, and entered inside to carefully inspect the body of Jesus. They wanted to know that His body was still there and that He was really dead, so that is what they did. They would have never sealed the tomb unless they had first conducted a full inspection and affirmed Jesus was there and that He was dead.

A Watch Was Requested

Yet this wasn't enough. The religious leaders *still* had doubts and continued asking for more security. Matthew 27:65 states, "Pilate said unto them, Ye have a watch: go your way, make it as sure as ye can." The word "watch" in Greek is the word *koustodia*, which describes *a guard or watch*. In the First Century, it pictured *a group of four Roman soldiers whose shift changed every three hours*. The shift frequently rotated to ensure the soldiers were alert and fully awake at all times. When Pilate said, "Ye have a watch," a better translation could read, *"Here. I'm giving you a set of soldiers. Take them and guard the tomb."*

Also note the word "sure" in verse 65. It is different than the word used in verse 64. Here, the word "sure" is the Greek word *asphalidzo*, which means *to provide added security* or *to assure that security is achieved*. "So they went, and made the sepulchre sure, sealing the stone, and setting a watch" (Matthew 27:66).

Dead and Buried

Make no mistake — Jesus was dead. The centurion who thrust his spear in Jesus' side saw the mixture of blood and water flow. This was confirmation of congestive heart failure. So the centurion verified Jesus was dead.

Next, Joseph of Arimathea and Nicodemus spent hours preparing Jesus' body for burial. Mary Magdalene and Mary the mother of Joseph were also present, assisting and gazing intently at Him. Clearly, there was no life left in His mangled form. If He had been alive, they would surely have known it.

Furthermore, the religious leaders along with Roman soldiers and officials from Pilate's court all thoroughly examined Jesus' body in the tomb and unequivocally confirmed He was dead. Romans knew about death; they were masters at inflicting it. Once they all verified the body was Jesus' and that He was dead, they rolled the burial stone back in place, and Pilate's representative sealed the tomb with the official seal of the Roman governor.

All these things legally authenticated that Jesus was dead.

STUDY QUESTIONS

> Study to shew thyself approved unto God, a workman that needeth
> not to be ashamed, rightly dividing the word of truth.
> — 2 Timothy 2:15

1. What new facts did you learn about Joseph of Arimathea who received the body of Jesus from Pilate, the preparation of Jesus' body for burial, and the people who were present when they laid Him to rest?
2. Before Pilate released Jesus' body to Joseph, what does Mark 15:43-45 say Pilate did first?
3. In your own words, explain what had to be done before Pilate's official seal could be placed on Jesus' tomb? What did the seal signify and how did it legally authenticate Jesus' death?

PRACTICAL APPLICATION

> But be ye doers of the word, and not hearers only,
> deceiving your own selves.
> — James 1:22

1. Immediately after Jesus surrendered His spirit, some amazing things took place in the temple and in Jerusalem. Read Matthew 27:51-55 and summarize what happened. If you had been in the city and had witnessed those events, what might have been your response?
2. Imagine you were at the scene with Joseph of Arimathea, Nicodemus, Mary Magdalene, and Mary the mother of Joseph, preparing Jesus' body for burial. What kind of thoughts and emotions might you have experienced?

LESSON 24

TOPIC
Behold, He Is Risen!

SCRIPTURES

1. **Matthew 28:1-6** — In the end of the sabbath, as it began to dawn toward the first day of the week, came Mary Magdalene and the other Mary to see the sepulchre. And, behold, there was a great earthquake... the angel of the Lord descended from heaven, and came and rolled back the stone from the door, and sat upon it. ...His countenance was like lightning, and his raiment white as snow.... And for fear of him the keepers did shake, and became as dead men. And the angel answered and said unto the women, Fear not ye: for I know that ye seek Jesus, which was crucified. He is not here: for he is risen, as he said. Come, see the place where the Lord lay.

2. **Mark 16:2-5** — And very early in the morning the first day of the week, they came unto the sepulchre at the rising of the sun. And they said among themselves, Who shall roll us away the stone from the door of the sepulchre? And when they looked, they saw that the stone was rolled away: for it was very great. And entering into the sepulchre, they saw a young man sitting on the right side, clothed in a long white garment; and they were affrighted.

3. **Luke 24:3-8** — And they entered in, and found not the body of the Lord Jesus. ...They were much perplexed thereabout....two men stood by them in shining garments. And as they were afraid, and bowed down their faces to the earth, they [the angels] said unto them, Why seek ye the living among the dead? He is not here, but is risen: remember how he spake unto you when he was yet in Galilee, saying, The Son of man must be delivered into the hands of sinful men, and be crucified, and the third day rise again. And they remembered his words.

4. **Mark 16:7,8** — But go your way, tell his disciples.... And they went out quickly, and fled from the sepulchre; for they trembled and were amazed....

5. **Matthew 28:8** — And they departed quickly from the sepulchre with fear and great joy; and did run to bring his disciples word.

6. **Luke 24:9-11** — And returned from the sepulchre, and told all these things unto the eleven, and to all the rest. It was Mary Magdalene, and Joanna, and Mary the mother of James, and other women that were with them, which told these things unto the apostles. And their words seemed to them as idle tales, and they believed them not.

GREEK WORDS

1. "behold" — (*idou*): perhaps better translated as, *Wow*; it pictures shock, amazement, and wonder
2. "great" — μ (*megas*): huge, massive, or enormous
3. "earthquake" — μ (*seismos*): a literal earthquake
4. "very" — (*sphodra*): very much; exceedingly; extremely
5. "sat" — μ (*kathemai*): to sit down
6. "countenance" — (*idea*): external appearance; sight
7. "lightning" — ϖ (*astrapto*): pictures something dazzling; shining or flashing like lightning
8. "raiment" — μ (*enduma*): clothing; an outer garment
9. "white" — (*leukos*): light, bright, brilliant; dazzlingly brilliant
10. "snow" — (*chion*): snow; a blinding white appearance, like sunshine on the snow
11. "fear" — (*phobos*): a panic-stricken fear; terror
12. "shake" — (*seio*): to shake; tremble; or quiver; to quake for fear
13. "dead" — (*nekros*): lifeless; pictures a lifeless corpse
14. "risen" — (*egeiro*): to arouse from death
15. "see" — (*horao*): to see; to behold; to perceive; to delightfully view; a scrutinizing look; to look with the intent to examine; to fully view; to experience; to know something from personal observation, not from secondhand information
16. "young man" — (*neaniskos*): a young man who is filled with vigor and energy and who is in the prime of his life; illustrates the vitality, strength, and ever-youthful appearance of angels
17. "clothed" — ϖ (*periballo*): a garment draped about his shoulders, as a mighty warrior or ruler would be dressed
18. "white" — (*leukos*): light, bright, brilliant; dazzlingly brilliant

19. "garment" — (*stole*): a long, flowing robe normally worn by royalty, commanders, kings, priests, and other elite individuals or those of high distinction
20. "affrighted" — μ μ (*ekthambeomai*): to be astonished; blown away; pictures a mind-boggling experience
21. "perplexed" — ϖ (*aporeo*): to lose one's way; pictures someone so confused that he can't figure out where he is, what he's doing, or what is happening around him; a person completely bewildered by events
22. "stood by" — μ (*ephistemi*): to come upon suddenly; to take by surprise; to burst upon the scene; to unexpectedly appear
23. "shining" — ϖ (*astrapto*): pictures something dazzling; shining or flashing like lightning
24. "garments" — (*esthes*): apparel; raiment; garments; a robe
25. "risen" — (*egeiro*): to arouse from death
26. "rise again" — (*anastenai*): to stand again; to stand back to life again; to rise up from the dead
27. "idle tales" — (*leros*): nonsense; babble; a state of delirium

SYNOPSIS

The Church of the Holy Sepulchre in Jerusalem commemorates the place where Jesus was buried, but more importantly, where He was raised from the dead. This historic site — which many scholars believe is the authentic tomb where Jesus was buried and resurrected — was first recognized in about 326 AD That is when the first church was built there. Today the tomb is empty because Jesus is not there! He was resurrected and is now seated at the right hand of God the Father in Heaven.

The emphasis of this lesson:

Jesus' resurrection from the dead is the foundation of our faith. Many witnessed His life after death. If there had been only the cross but no resurrection, our faith would be in vain. However, because there was a resurrection and Jesus is alive, we have a future and a hope in Him!

Women Were Witnesses to Christ's Resurrection

A group of devoted women were among the first to witness the resurrection. Matthew 28:1 says, "In the end of the sabbath, as it began to dawn toward the first day of the week, came Mary Magdalene and the other Mary to see the sepulchre." Luke 24:10 confirms this, adding that Joanna and other women were with the two Marys. They went to the tomb to anoint the body of Jesus.

Jewish custom and culture required that the body of the deceased be anointed with spices and ointments. These were prepared by the women in their homes and then carried to the burial site to administer to Jesus' body. They didn't know that the tomb had been inspected by the religious leaders and Roman soldiers and then legally sealed by Pilate's authorities. Nor were they aware that Roman soldiers had been posted to guard Jesus' body.

What these women did know was that they needed someone to roll away the stone. Mark 16:2 and 3 says, "And very early in the morning the first day of the week, they came unto the sepulchre at the rising of the sun. And they said among themselves, Who shall roll us away the stone from the door of the sepulchre? And when they looked, they saw that the stone was [already] rolled away: for it was very great."

The Stone Was Rolled Away!

The morning of Jesus' resurrection, Matthew 28:2 says, "And, behold, there was a great earthquake: for the angel of the Lord descended from heaven, and came and rolled back the stone from the door, and sat upon it."

First, notice it says, "Behold, there was a great earthquake...." The word "behold" is the Greek word *idou*, which conveys *intense emotion* and would perhaps better translated as, *Wow!* It pictures *shock, amazement, and wonder.* That is what these women were feeling in that moment. When they saw the stone rolled away, they were totally bewildered.

Second, there was a "great earthquake." The word "great" is the Greek word *megas*, meaning *huge, massive,* or *enormous.* The word "earthquake" is from the Greek word *seismos*, which is *a literal earthquake.* This was an enormous, massive, earthshaking event that took place on that morning.

Next, we see that it was the angel of the Lord that was responsible for rolling back the stone from the door. Mark 16:4 adds, "And when they looked, they saw that the stone was rolled away: for it was very great." The word "very" in Greek is the word *sphodra*, which describes *something that is exceedingly or extremely great*. And the word "great" is again the Greek word *megas*, meaning *huge*, *massive*, or *enormous*. The stone at the entrance to the tomb was enormous, yet the angel managed to move it out of the way.

Looking back at Matthew 28:2, we see that after the angel moved the massive stone, he "sat upon it." The word "sat" is the Greek word *kathemai*, which means *to sit down*. The fact that the angel could move such a massive stone indicates how powerful he was, and the fact that he turned the enormous stone into a chair denotes that the angel was likely huge in size.

Angels Were Also Witnesses to Christ's Resurrection

The first witnesses to the resurrection of Jesus were angels. We've just seen that one came from Heaven and rolled away the massive stone at the entrance to the tomb and sat down on it. Matthew 28:3 describes what this angel looked like, saying, "His countenance was like lightning, and his raiment white as snow."

The word "countenance" is the Greek word *idea*, which describes *external appearance* or *what you can see with your eyes*. The angel's appearance was like "lightning" — the Greek word *astrapto*, which pictures *something dazzling, shining, or flashing like lightning*.

Matthew went on to say his "raiment" was "white as snow." The word "raiment" is the Greek word *enduma*, which describes *clothing or an outer garment*. The angel's clothing was "white," which is the Greek word *leukos*. This denotes *something light, bright, brilliant, or dazzlingly brilliant*. His clothing was as white as "snow" — the Greek word *chion*, which describes *snow that has a blinding white appearance*. It is *the picture of sun shining on the snow so brightly that it's blinding*.

So the angel sitting on the massive entrance stone had a dazzlingly brilliant appearance. It was so bright, it was like the midday sun reflecting off snow. The women could hardly look at him because he was so blinding.

The Soldiers Became as 'Dead Men'

Meanwhile, as the great earthquake hit and the angel descended and rolled away the enormous entrance stone, the four soldiers who were stationed to keep watch were present at the scene. Upon seeing the angel and his brilliantly blinding appearance and size, the Bible says, "…For fear of him the keepers did shake, and became as dead men" (Matthew 28:4).

First, it says, "For fear of him." The word "fear" is the Greek word *phobos*, which describes *a panic-stricken fear or terror*. These men were having a major panic attack and began to "shake." The word "shake" is the Greek word *seio*, which means *to shake, tremble, quiver, or quake with fear*.

Then the Bible says they "became as dead men." The word "dead" is taken from the Greek word *nekros*, which pictures *a lifeless corpse*. These strong, burly, well-trained military men were paralyzed with fear at the sight of this angel. They fell to the ground under the power of God as if they were dead. These soldiers had been through many battles, but they had never experienced anything like this.

Eventually, they managed to get up from the ground and make their way into the city to report the happenings to the chief priests (*see* Matthew 28:11) — but not before seeing with their eyes and hearing with their ears the conversation the angel had with the women at the tomb.

Angels, Angels Everywhere!

Angel #1 — Sitting Atop the Stone

The women stood in amazement and shock, their eyes riveted upon the dazzlingly brilliant and strong angel sitting atop the large entrance stone. As the guards lay paralyzed on the ground, the angel said unto the women, "…Fear not ye: for I know that ye seek Jesus, which was crucified. He is not here: for he is risen, as he said. Come, see the place where the Lord lay" (Matthew 28:5, 6).

First, notice the angel said, "He is risen." The word "risen" is from the Greek word *egeiro*, which means *to arouse from death*. Jesus had been aroused from death itself. The angel then said, "Come, see the place where the Lord lay." The word "see" is a translation of the Greek word *horao*, which means *to see; to behold; to perceive; to delightfully view; to take a scrutinizing look; to look with the intent to examine; to fully view; or to experience*. It carries the idea of *knowing something from personal observation, not from secondhand information*.

When the angel said, "Come, see," he was saying, "Hey, come take a good look at this for yourselves. Examine the place where Jesus was laid. Scrutinize it carefully. We want you to have a firsthand view, not secondhand information." So the women accepted the angel's invitation to look inside.

Angel #2 — Sitting Where Jesus Lay

Luke 24:3 says the women "…entered in, and found not the body of the Lord Jesus." Mark 16:5 continues by saying, "And entering into the sepulchre, they saw a young man sitting on the right side, clothed in a long white garment; and they were affrightened." This was another angel.

Mark's account reveals that the angel appeared as a "young man" — the Greek word *neaniskos*. This describes *a young man who is filled with vigor and energy and who is in the prime of his life*. This word illustrates *the vitality, strength, and ever-youthful appearance of angels*.

It also says the angel was "clothed in a long white garment." The word "clothed" is the Greek word *periballo*, which describes *a garment draped about the shoulders, as a mighty warrior or ruler would be dressed*. The garment was "white," which is translated from the Greek word *leukos*, meaning *light, bright, brilliant*, or *dazzlingly brilliant*.

Finally, we see the word "garment," which is the Greek word *stole*. This describes *a long, flowing robe normally worn by royalty, commanders, kings, priests, and other elite individuals or those of high distinction*.

When the women saw this second angel, they were "affrightened." The Greek word for "affrightened" means *to be astonished or blown away*. It denotes *a mind-boggling experience*. The sight of this angel defied their senses and their intellects. They were *blown away* by what they were experiencing!

Luke 24:4 says the women were "much perplexed." The word "perplexed" is the Greek word *aporeo*, which means *to lose one's way*. It pictures *someone so confused that he can't figure out where he is, what he's doing, or what is happening around him; the person is completely bewildered by the events taking place*.

When you consider all these women had seen since they arrived at the tomb, you can see how they would be perplexed in exactly this way.

Angels #3 and #4 — Standing Beside Them

As the women stood inside the sepulcher trying to take it all in, Luke 24:4 says, "…Behold, two men stood by them in shining garments." In that moment, two more angels materialized and "stood by them." The phrase "stood by" is the Greek word *ephistemi*, which means *to come upon sud-*

denly, to take by surprise, to burst upon the scene, or to suddenly or unexpectedly appear.

The account continues in Luke 24:5-8:

> And as they were afraid, and bowed down their faces to the earth, they [the angels] said unto them, Why seek ye the living among the dead? He is not here, but is risen: remember how he spake unto you when he was yet in Galilee, saying, The Son of man must be delivered into the hands of sinful men, and be crucified, and the third day rise again. And they remembered his words.

Twice in this passage the angels say, "He is risen" — the word "risen" from the Greek word *egeiro*, which means *to arouse from death*. They also reminded the women what Jesus had told them — that He would "rise again" on the third day. The phrase "rise again" is the Greek word *anastenai*, which means *to stand again, to stand back to life or to rise from the dead*. Jesus Christ had "stand again" power! And that same "stand again" power lives in you and me today!

'Go Quickly and Tell!'

Once the angels had declared to the women that Jesus had risen, they instructed them to go and inform the disciples of the great news of His resurrection. Three of the gospels include this scene:

Matthew 28:7 and 8 says, "And go quickly, and tell his disciples that he is risen from the dead.... And they departed quickly from the sepulchre with fear and great joy; and did run to bring his disciples word."

Mark 16:7 and 8 says, "But go your way, tell his disciples.... And they went out quickly, and fled from the sepulchre; for they trembled and were amazed...."

Luke 24:9-11 says, "And returned from the sepulchre, and told all these things unto the eleven, and to all the rest. It was Mary Magdalene, and Joanna, and Mary the mother of James, and other women that were with them, which told these things unto the apostles. And their words seemed to them as idle tales, and they believed them not."

Notice in Luke's account that the news the women shared seemed like "idle tales" to the disciples. "Idle tales" is the Greek word *leros*, which means *nonsense, babble*, or *a state of delirium*. When the women showed up to tell all that they had seen and heard, they were excited and a bit delirious. With their emotions and thoughts firing at full speed in different directions, they probably weren't able to communicate very effectively.

Nevertheless, their witness sparked a fire in the hearts of the disciples. Peter and John were so stirred by what they heard, they ran to the tomb to see for themselves what had happened to Jesus. The women's witness lets us know we don't need to worry about trying to perfectly present the Gospel. We just need to pray and share the best that we can. The Holy Spirit will do the rest.

STUDY QUESTIONS

Study to shew thyself approved unto God, a workman that needeth not to be ashamed, rightly dividing the word of truth.
— 2 Timothy 2:15

1. The gospels record amazing things that took place in and around the tomb of Jesus. What new details did you learn about these events and those that were present the morning of the resurrection?
2. What happened to the guards who saw the angel roll away the stone and heard him speak to the women about Jesus who was no longer in the tomb? Read Matthew 28:11-15 for the answer.

PRACTICAL APPLICATION

But be ye doers of the word, and not hearers only, deceiving your own selves.
— James 1:22

1. Acts 1:3 says after Jesus had risen from the grave, He showed Himself to His disciples and many others for a period of 40 days. In what ways has the Lord "shown" Himself to you by His Word and His Spirit to establish, strengthen, and steady you in your faith and your service to Him?
2. The morning of Jesus' resurrection, He appeared to two of His disciples, listening and talking with them. But they didn't recognize Him because they were very discouraged. Pause and pray: "Lord, in what areas of my life am I blinded to Your presence?" Be still and listen.

What is He saying? Invite Him into those situations, receiving the wisdom and strength He provides.

LESSON 25

TOPIC
An Empty Tomb!

SCRIPTURES

1. **Matthew 28:5, 6** — And the angel answered and said unto the women, Fear not ye: for I know that ye seek Jesus, which was crucified. He is not here: for he is risen, as he said. Come, see the place where the Lord lay.
2. **Luke 24:3-8** — And they entered in, and found not the body of the Lord Jesus. ...they were much perplexed thereabout...two men stood by them in shining garments. And as they were afraid, and bowed down their faces to the earth, they [the angels] said unto them, Why seek ye the living among the dead? He is not here, but is risen: remember how he spake unto you when he was yet in Galilee, saying, The Son of man must be delivered into the hands of sinful men, and be crucified, and the third day rise again. And they remembered his words.
3. **Luke 24:9-12** — ...told these things unto the apostles. And their words seemed to them as idle tales, and they believed them not. ... departed, wondering in himself at that which was come to pass.
4. **Mark 16:5** — And entering into the sepulchre, they saw a young man sitting on the right side, clothed in a long white garment; and they were affrighted.
5. **Mark 16:7, 8** — But go your way, tell his disciples.... And they went out quickly, and fled from the sepulchre....
6. **Matthew 28:8** — ...did run to bring his disciples word.
7. **John 20:3, 4** — Peter therefore went forth, and that other disciple, and came to the sepulchre. So they ran both together: and the other disciple [John] did outrun Peter, and came first to the sepulchre.
8. **John 20:5** — And he stooping down, and looking in, saw the linen clothes lying; yet went he not in.

9. **John 20:6-8** — Then cometh Simon Peter following him, and went into the sepulchre, and seeth the linen clothes lie, and the napkin, that was about his head, not lying with the linen clothes, but wrapped together in a place by itself. Then went in also that other disciple, which came first to the sepulchre, and he saw, and believed.

GREEK WORDS

1. "risen" — (*egeiro*): to arouse from death
2. "see" — (*horao*): to see; to behold; to perceive; to delightfully view; a scrutinizing look; to look with the intent to examine; to fully view; to experience; to know something from personal observation, not from secondhand information
3. "young man" — (*neaniskos*): a young man who is filled with vigor and energy and who is in the prime of his life; illustrates the vitality, strength, and ever-youthful appearance of angels
4. "clothed" — ϖ (*periballo*): pictures a garment draped about one's shoulders, as a mighty warrior or ruler would wear
5. "white" — (*leukos*): light, bright, brilliant; dazzlingly brilliant
6. "garment" — (*stole*): a long, flowing robe normally worn by royalty, commanders, kings, priests, and other elite individuals or those of high distinction
7. "affrighted" — μ μ (*ekthambeomai*): astonished; blown away; pictures a mind-boggling experience
8. "perplexed" — ϖ (*aporeo*): to lose one's way; pictures someone so confused that he can't figure out where he is, what he's doing, or what is happening around him; a person completely bewildered by events
9. "stood by" — μ (*ephistemi*): to come upon suddenly; to take by surprise; to burst upon the scene; to unexpectedly appear
10. "shining" — ϖ (*astrapto*): pictures something dazzling; shining or flashing like lightning
11. "garments" — (*esthes*): apparel; raiment; garments; a robe
12. "rise again" — (*anastenai*): to stand again; to stand back to life again; to arise from the dead
13. "idle tales" — (*leros*): nonsense; babble; a state of delirium

14. "stooping down" — ϖ ϖ (*parakupto*): to peer into; to bend low to take a closer look; to stoop down to see something better; to look intently; to examine closely
15. "saw" — ϖ (*blepo*): to watch, to see, or to be aware; often jolted and jarred a viewer to perk up and pay attention to what is being seen
16. "linen clothes" — (*othonion*): extremely expensive materials usually produced in Egypt; expensive wrappings; nobles paid high prices to have garments made from this material
17. "seeth" — μ (*theaomai*): pictures a theater; to look, like a patron who attends a play and carefully watches every act, and listens attentively to every word because he doesn't want to miss anything important; to observe the entire scene, analyzing the whole scenario displayed before you
18. "napkin" — (*soudarion*): a burial cloth placed upon the face of the dead at burial
19. "wrapped" — (*entulisso*): to neatly fold; to nicely arrange; or to arrange in an orderly fashion

SYNOPSIS

The Church of the Holy Sepulchre in Jerusalem is believed by many to be the historically authenticated site of Christ's burial and resurrection. This is where many scholars believe His body was actually laid more than 2,000 years ago. Likewise, it is also believed to be the very stone-hewn tomb in which the power of God entered into the body of Jesus and miraculously aroused Him from death and restored Him to life! A church was built on this site and was officially recognized in 326 AD by Emperor Constantine to commemorate these miraculous acts. And that empty tomb is still there today!

The emphasis of this lesson:

Women were among the first to witness the empty tomb and experience supernatural encounters with angels. Peter and John also saw the empty grave. John walked away believing; Peter walked away questioning until later when Christ proved He had risen by appearing to His disciples on multiple occasions.

'Come and See!'

Early in the morning on the first day of the week, Mary Magdalene, Joanna, and Mary the mother of James all came to the tomb where Jesus had been laid. Much to their surprise, the entrance stone had been rolled away, and an angel was sitting on top of it. "And the angel answered and said unto the women, Fear not ye: for I know that ye seek Jesus, which was crucified. He is not here: for he is risen, as he said. Come, see the place where the Lord lay" (Matthew 28:5, 6).

Here is a review of some of what we learned in the last lesson: The word "risen" is the Greek word *egeiro*, which means *to arouse from death*. Though dead in the presence of many witnesses, Jesus was aroused from death as if He had only been sleeping! He was no longer physically present in the tomb when the women arrived.

The angel then invited the women to come and "see" inside the grave. The word "see" is the Greek word *horao*, which means *to see, to behold, to perceive*, or *to delightfully view*. It describes *a scrutinizing look; to look with the intent to examine; to fully view; to experience or to know something from personal observation, not from secondhand information.*

When the angel said, "Come and see," he was really saying, *"Come and delightfully view the place where Jesus once laid. We want you to experience and perceive this with your own eyes and examine everything with a scrutinizing look. We want you to know what has happened from personal observation, not secondhand information."*

Meeting the 'Young Man' Clothed in White

Upon entering the sepulcher, Luke 24:3 says the women "…found not the body of the Lord Jesus." Mark 16:5 tells us "…they saw a young man sitting on the right side, clothed in a long white garment; and they were affrighted." This "young man" was another angel. Several words in the next verse confirm this.

For instance, the phrase "young man" is the Greek word *neaniskos*, which describes *a young man who is filled with vigor and energy and who is in the prime of his life*. It also illustrates *the vitality, strength, and ever-youthful appearance of angels.*

"Clothed" is the Greek word *periballo*, and it pictures *a garment draped about one's shoulders, as a mighty warrior or ruler would wear*. Its color was "white," which is the Greek word *leukos*, describing *something light, bright, brilliant, or dazzlingly brilliant*. The next word is "garment," which is the Greek word *stole*. This describes *a long, flowing robe normally worn by royalty, commanders, kings, priests, and other elite individuals or those of high distinction*.

When the women saw this vibrant, regally attired angel sitting to the right of where Jesus' body had lain, they were "affrightened" (Mark 16:5). This means they were *astonished and blown away*; it was *a mind-boggling experience*. In fact, it was so mind-boggling that Luke 24:4 says they were "perplexed." The word "perplexed" is the Greek word *aporeo*, which means *to lose one's way*. It pictures *someone so confused that he can't figure out where he is, what he's doing, or what is happening around him*. He is *completely bewildered by the surrounding events*.

Encountering 'Two Men' in Shining Garments

There they were — a group of devoted women who had come to the tomb to anoint the body of Jesus with spices as Jewish culture and custom dictated. After encountering two angels — one on the outside of the tomb and one on the inside — they were mentally and emotionally "lost" by the unexpected, mind-boggling events they were experiencing.

Then Luke 24:4 says, "…Behold, two men stood by them in shining garments." The words "stood by" is the Greek word *ephistemi*, which means *to come upon suddenly; to take by surprise; to burst upon the scene*; or *to unexpectedly appear*. These "two men" were two more angels, and they were dressed in "shining garments." The word "shining" is the Greek word *astrapto*, which pictures *something dazzling, shining, or flashing like lightning*. The word "garments" is the Greek word *esthes*, and it describes *apparel, raiment, garments*, or *a long, flowing robe*.

Luke 24:5-7 says the women "…were afraid, and bowed their faces to the earth, they [the angels] said unto them, Why seek ye the living among the dead? He is not here, but is risen: remember how he spake unto you when he was yet in Galilee, saying, The Son of man must be delivered into the hands of sinful men, and be crucified, and the third day rise again."

The word "risen" is again the Greek word *egeiro*, meaning *to arouse from death*. The phrase "rise again" in verse 7 is the Greek word *anastenai*, which means *to stand again or to stand back to life*. It describes *resurrection from the dead*! Resurrection power is "stand again" power! It is what Jesus had that brought Him back to life, and it's the same power *you* have in Him to restore you and stand you up on your feet again.

The Women Were Among the First Witnesses of Christ and His Power

When the angels explained why Jesus' body was no longer there, the women remembered Jesus' words — that He would "rise again" on the third day. Immediately, the angels said, "But go your way, tell his disciples and Peter that he goeth before you into Galilee.... And they went out quickly, and fled from the sepulchre; for they trembled and were amazed…" (Mark 16:7, 8). This is affirmed in Matthew 28:7 and 8 as well as in Luke 24:8-10.

In Luke 24:11, we see the disciples' response to the witness of the women. "And their words seemed to them as idle tales, and they believed them not." The phrase "idle tales" is the Greek word *leros*, which describes *nonsense*, *babble*, or *a state of delirium*. After seeing and hearing all that they had experienced, the women were "perplexed" (*aporeo*) — they had mentally and emotionally lost their way. And because they didn't fully comprehend what they had just witnessed, their confusion came across in their communication.

Nevertheless, what the women shared was enough to light a fire of curiosity in Peter and John. John 20:3 and 4 says, "Peter therefore went forth, and that other disciple, and came to the sepulchre. So they ran both together: and the other disciple did outrun Peter, and came first to the sepulchre."

Peter and John Ran to the Sepulcher

Peter and John were desperate to see what the women were trying to communicate. They were the only two disciples to go to the tomb. For whatever reason, the others didn't move. As a result, they missed out on a divine moment that would never come their way again.

John arrived at the sepulcher first. "And he stooping down, and looking in, saw the linen clothes lying; yet went he not in" (John 20:5). Notice the phrase "stooping down." It comes from the Greek word *parakupto*, which means *to peer into, to bend low to take a closer look, to stoop down to see something better, to look intently, or to examine closely.* That's what John did. He bent down low and peered into the tomb with an examining eye, where he "saw" the linen clothes.

The word "saw" is from the Greek word *blepo*, which in this case indicates *something that jolts and jars a viewer to reality.* It means *to perk up and pay attention to what is being seen.* When John "saw" the "linen clothes," he knew something significant had taken place. The words "linen clothes" is the Greek word *othonion*, which describes *extremely expensive materials usually produced in Egypt.* These were expensive wrappings. Wealthy people paid high prices to have garments made from this material.

Remember, it was Joseph of Arimathea who had buried the body of Jesus in his own tomb that had never been used, and Nicodemus had assisted him. Joseph was a man of substantial wealth, and the use of the word *othonion* ("linen clothes") tells us that *Joseph gave his very best to Jesus.* When he and Nicodemus buried Christ, they didn't bury Him as a poor man. They laid Him to rest as a rich man — giving Him the honor of a rich man's tomb and a rich man's clothing. Their passionate love for Jesus was displayed in their extravagant investment at His burial.

Two Disciples — Two Different Responses

When John arrived, he didn't rush into the tomb. Initially, he remained outside. Graves were highly respected. Perhaps that is why he hesitated. On the other hand, maybe John saw Pilate's broken seal and realized that the tomb had become a crime scene. Pilate's seal meant that no one was authorized to enter the tomb. To go inside posed the possibility of risking his reputation and ending up in serious trouble. More than likely, thoughts like these were running through John's mind.

John 20:6 and 7 says, "Then cometh Simon Peter following him, and went into the sepulchre, and seeth the linen clothes lie, and the napkin, that was about his head, not lying with the linen clothes, but wrapped together in a place by itself."

The word "seeth" in verse 6 is the Greek word *theaomai*, which pictures *a theater.* It means *to look, like a patron who attends a play and carefully watches every act, and listens attentively to every word because he doesn't want to miss anything important.* That is what Peter did. He observed the entire scene, analyzing everything displayed before him — including the "napkin."

This word "napkin" is the Greek word *soudarion*, which describes *a burial cloth placed upon the face of the dead at burial*. The Bible says this napkin was "wrapped together in a place by itself." The term "wrapped" is the Greek word *entulisso*, which means *to neatly fold, to nicely arrange, or to arrange in an orderly fashion*. After Jesus had been aroused from death, he took the time to nicely fold the napkin that had covered His face, signifying His commitment to doing things decently and in order.

John 20:8 says, "Then went in also that other disciple, which came first to the sepulchre, and he saw, and believed." When John finally went inside and saw everything up close, he believed Jesus had risen from the dead. Peter's response was different. Luke 24:12 says that after he went in the tomb and saw everything, he "…departed, wondering in himself at that which was come to pass." John left *believing*, and Peter left *questioning*.

Shortly thereafter, Jesus appeared to all the disciples, again and again, giving proof of His resurrection from the dead. The reason the tomb was and still is empty is *Jesus is alive*! That is what we celebrate as believers in Christ.

Why not step out of your comfort zone and witness to someone else about His resurrection power and His sacrifice to save us to the uttermost? Can you think of anything better than seeing someone surrender his life to Christ and make Him Lord of his life?

STUDY QUESTIONS

> Study to shew thyself approved unto God, a workman that needeth not to be ashamed, rightly dividing the word of truth.
> — 2 Timothy 2:15

1. Upon hearing from the women that Jesus was no longer in the tomb, Peter and John ran to the grave to see for themselves. The other disciples didn't move. What do you think may have caused them to stay put? If you had been one of the nine who stayed behind, what would you have needed to hear to light a fire in you to go after Jesus?
2. The same Spirit that raised Christ from the dead lives in *you*! (*See* Romans 8:11.) Second Corinthians 3:16-18 and Ephesians 3:16-20 talk about the Spirit's work in you. What is the Lord showing you in these verses? Take a minute to pray, inviting the Holy Spirit to release

His power in *every* area of your life — including the areas you may have previously withheld.
3. Clearly, Peter and John went after Jesus and experienced a divine encounter that the other disciples missed. What might *going after Jesus* look like in a person's life today? (Consider Psalm 27:4-8; 105:4; Isaiah 55:6; Matthew 6:33; 11:28-30; James 4:7-10; Hebrews 10:22-25.)

PRACTICAL APPLICATION

> But be ye doers of the word, and not hearers only, deceiving your own selves.
> —James 1:22

1. Be honest. Are you *going after Jesus*? If not, what is holding you back? What can you do today to move toward Him and begin experiencing all that He has planned for you?
2. Joseph of Arimathea gave Jesus *his very best* — providing Him with a rich man's clothes and a rich man's tomb. Ask yourself, *Am I giving Jesus my very best? Is there an area in my life where I know I can do better? If so, where? What specifically can I do right now to come up higher?*

www.ingramcontent.com/pod-product-compliance
Lightning Source LLC
Chambersburg PA
CBHW051838090426
42736CB00011B/1861